Falling
into
Now

Memories of Sport,
Traumatic Brain Injury, and Education

Claire Smith

◖iUniverse®

FALLING INTO NOW
MEMORIES OF SPORT, TRAUMATIC BRAIN
INJURY, AND EDUCATION

iUniverse Star
an iUniverse LLC imprint

iUniverse books may be ordered through booksellers or by contacting:

iUniverse
1663 Liberty Drive
Bloomington, IN 47403
www.iuniverse.com
1-800-Authors (1-800-288-4677)

Because of the dynamic nature of the Internet, any web addresses or links contained in this book may have changed since publication and may no longer be valid. The views expressed in this work are solely those of the author and do not necessarily reflect the views of the publisher, and the publisher hereby disclaims any responsibility for them.

Any people depicted in stock imagery provided by Thinkstock are models, and such images are being used for illustrative purposes only. Certain stock imagery © Thinkstock.

ISBN: 978-1-5320-6040-3 (sc)
ISBN: 978-1-5320-6046-5 (e)

Library of Congress Control Number: 2017913770

Print information available on the last page.

iUniverse rev. date: 10/18/2018

For my incredible parents,

Brad and Renée Smith,

who are there for me

Now

Contents

A Quick Word

It took months of arranging and rearranging before I settled on how best to organise this memoir. I've scattered short chapters called *Now* throughout the text; in them, I reflect on the preceding stories. The purpose of the introductory *Now* is, however, a bit different. In it, I show readers that I haven't given up trying to preserve the memories of my equestrian life, even though it's becoming more and more difficult for me to do so. The memories of that cherished past still echo off the walls of my heart, albeit faintly.

The first *Now* leads into the section Horses, so it's understandable if you suspect this memoir is all about my equestrian experiences. However, I only recount these memories in the first few chapters. I've kept my stories from that life to a minimum. Most of the ones I've chosen to share illustrate my single-mindedness, dedication and attention to every detail. These traits are essential for anyone who is reaching for the top of any sport—and, as I was forced to discover, when recovering from severe injury.

Horses ends abruptly on September 13, 1997. The sections that follow are named Chaos, Restitution and Quest, after the three types of illness narratives introduced by Arthur Frank, professor emeritus at the University of Calgary. Because this memoir exemplifies Frank's typology, I thought it appropriate to use his illness narrative types as section titles. Frank does feel, however, that during any illness these types of narratives are "told, alternatively and repeatedly … [they] are like patterns in a kaleidoscope: for a moment, the different colours are given one specific form, then the tube shifts and another form emerges."[1]

Frank suggests that each story's positioning should be considered fluid. As you read the memoir, a story's location on the spectrum of illness narrative types—chaos, restitution or quest—may shift, depending on how you interpret the story.

For the four months immediately following September 13, 1997, post-traumatic amnesia, or PTA – the inability to store new memories – ruled my world. Because I remember nothing of those months, I've told the stories under Chaos (the section immediately following September 13, 1997), using my parents' voices. Post-traumatic amnesia began to retreat in the middle of January 1998, so the point of view becomes mine again, and it remains so for the rest of the memoir.

I'll always appreciate Laurel Richardson's and Elizabeth Adams St. Pierre's words: "writing *is* thinking, writing *is* analysis, writing *is* indeed a seductive and tangled *method* of discovery."[2] It took two years after September 13, 1997, before I became cognitively able to, and found it therapeutic to, unravel and spill onto the page my tangled memories of those painful times. When I rearranged the disorganized mess of memories into cohesive paragraphs, I discovered much about myself. It was in no small part due to my writing that I was eventually able to reconcile the scrambled emotions that resulted from those turbulent years.

Only recently did I feel ready to revisit my memories of life as I'd lived it before September 13, 1997. Once again, I discovered as I wrote, learning much about myself as I reminisced about my life with horses. Finally, I felt ready to peacefully tuck away the memories of who I had once been.

After life-changing injury or illness, individuals may choose to wallow in self-pity and never move beyond the shattering impact that such an event can have on their lives. Or, as I did, though it took me many years, they can decide to learn from their traumatic experiences and incorporate what they've gone through into their constantly evolving selves. People's selves are never static; they are continually being recomposed. What people believe or think at any given moment will be integrated into who they are becoming. As individuals' lives move forward, their experiences in life, good and bad, keep contributing to their ongoing growth as human beings.

On the first page of Arthur Frank's memoir recounting his experiences with cancer, he expresses what I only discovered when I was almost finished writing my own memoir:

> *Illness takes away parts of your life, but in doing*
> *so it gives you the opportunity to choose the life*
> *you will lead, as opposed to living out the one*
> *you have simply accumulated over the years.*[3]

I'll never completely let go of the successes—or the crushing disappointments—that accentuated my time in the equestrian world. However, although I'll always miss those cherished years, this book is about so much more. It's about being driven to pursue a goal. It's about life-changing loss. It's about arduous recovery. It's about a life evolving into something completely unexpected.

Now

Early April
Merrickville, Ontario

The memories of my equestrian past have faded. They're drifting softly away as time relentlessly soldiers on, the last 19 years having eroded my ability to recall them. Like carefully saved old family photos, the memories' edges are soft and worn from years of touching, their images black and white. They've become just quick recollections of a most precious period of my life.

I couldn't bear it if the memories of those cherished years were to disappear forever, slipping permanently into my unconsciousness, becoming irretrievable. So, in order to keep them alive, I cling to the small moments that still visit me, albeit infrequently. Because these recollections of my past are bare and unadorned, I dress them, providing them with many details. Molding the memories into stories lets me enjoy those times again and again. On rare occasions, old reel movies play in my mind. Inevitably, as the years have gone by, the movies have become silent, Chaplin-like.

There—that's a start. Stretching my arms up and yawning, I swivel my desk chair away from my computer screen and gaze out the window at the snow. Some years, an early-April day such as this one hints of spring. Today, however, there's still plenty of snow on the ground. It sparkles defiantly in the sun, thanks to a thin layer of ice laid down by the freezing rain last week.

Even during these frosty months, when each day seems to struggle to wake up, my home office is alive with light. The office invigorates me, its brightness defying the inhospitable weather that peeks in through the white horizontal blinds. Daylight pours in through generous skylights that, while connecting the room to the sky, leave the brisk early-spring weather barricaded outside. Enormous windows boldly interrupt the red-wine paint on the walls, bringing more of the outdoors in. The paint colour, *caliente*, is described in brochures as hot, passionate and sexy. I just like the way it adds vibrancy and energy to my space.

Annie, a purebred mixed terrier from the local SPCA, sees my chair move and, reacting instantly, runs to the door. I can't hear myself think through her high-pitched, piercing barking.

"Okay, all right." I tell her. Awkwardly—the right leg of my jeans is covered from ankle to hip by a brace—I make my way across the room to where Annie is bouncing impatiently next to the terrace door, hardly able to contain herself. The brace is a lifesaver. When I sit, it allows my leg to bend normally; when I stand, it stops my right knee from painfully bending backwards. Years ago, I never imagined a day when I'd be grateful to be able to walk only a few steps or manage just a very short flight of stairs.

Pulling the door open, I enjoy watching my dog as she dashes out and punches down through the shiny ice, losing her legs in a massive snowbank. Annie seems oblivious to the frigid air that blasts by her and gusts effortlessly through the open door into my warm space. Slamming the door closed against the weather, I leave the dog outside for a moment and plunk myself inelegantly onto the old couch that faces the wood stove.

Inelegant is now normal; plunking is now normal. Finally I'm okay, I'm happy with how things are and who I *Now* am. When I suddenly had become unable to live life the only way I knew how, I'd spent the next few years constantly looking backwards, reliving every memory of my past with my horses. I had refused to let go of my past. Instead,

I'd yearned for the person I used to be and I'd clung to the singular, narrowly focused identity of "equestrian athlete." Since my teenage years, it was the only identity I'd acknowledged.

At long last I'm emotionally healthier. The past no longer scratches me painfully with each passing day. But although it's been more than 19 years since my life changed so dramatically, I still grasp at the disappearing memories of the time when I lived for my horses. They've become healthy, fond thoughts of a beloved period of my life; I'm now able to peacefully enjoy the fading, precious memories of my life with horses.

Because it's been so long, I'm surprised—startled even—when nostalgic memories of the past push their way into my consciousness. I always wonder how they choose when they'll appear in the *Now* of my life. I could be driving my car, taking out the garbage or feeding the dog. Suddenly my past will poke insistently at my *Now*, vying for attention, demanding that the *Now* stops in its tracks. Welcoming its intrusion, I can't help but immerse myself.

Occasionally, memories pounce on me when I'm sitting at my desk in front of my computer, waiting for inspiration. Then my fingers can't stop typing.

Riding in the early morning, the mist hovering, not yet burned away by the sun. Sitting on my faithful friend Gordon, his ears pricked, framing his world. Mine too, during that magical time.

Although I don't want the past to disappear completely, I do heed the words of Joan Didion, who writes that as time passes, "Memory fades, memory adjusts, memory conforms to what we think we remember."[4] I wonder how my memories have changed. Have they adjusted or adapted? Maybe the memories of my past have been redesigned in my dreams to conform to what I want to remember, how I want to remember.

For the first few years after my life suddenly changed, I absolutely would not acknowledge that there were many parts of my former life that I didn't miss at all. During the early years of my recovery, there's no way that I would have faced that harsh, unpleasant reality, let alone accept it. Instead, I continually struggled to turn back time, to be the person I used to be. It took years, but I finally admitted to myself that I was no longer wistful for the tough parts of those years, the relentless hard work. The aching tiredness, the frustration. I can certainly do without the tough realities that made up a large percentage of that time. I now question why on earth the very occasional flashes of success seemed to make it all worthwhile. At long last, I've put the loss of my former life in perspective.

Hypnotized by the flames as they tease and then devour the logs, I could easily sit next to the wood stove all day. Today might well be one of those days when I'm finished early. I might just not be inspired to remember, to write any longer. When memories aren't pressuring me, but I still feel that I must write something, my compositions seem stagnant, like gloomy old ponds. Recollections stay just out of reach, treading water in my mind's murky depth.

I need to go back to work. Closing the stove's flue to temper its fire, I transfer to my wheelchair and then let Annie in. When I return to my desk, words dangle just out of reach, challenging me to arrange them. Shifting my gaze away from the uninspiring computer screen, I become absorbed in the eight-by-ten photos mounted on the wall behind my desk. Pictures of my horses flow upwards before curving right to frame a window. It doesn't take long before each one triggers a chain of memories, squeezing aside any thoughts I might have had on what I should be doing.

HORSES

Somewhere behind the athlete you've become, and the hours of practice, and the coaches who have pushed you, is a little girl who fell in love with the game and never looked back.[5]

Beginnings

The Farm

In 1963, my parents bought a dilapidated stone house and 150 acres on the Rideau River outside the village of Burritts Rapids, Ontario. The house was structurally sound but only barely habitable. Initially, they rented an apartment in Ottawa. After a year of driving back and forth, Mom and Dad realized that the farm required far too much work to be only a weekend retreat, so the farm became their full-time residence.

My father is "Cruddums" to me. He always used to say, "Oh crud *this*, oh crud *that*" or "crudballs." When I was about 8, the monster Sweetums appeared on a Sesame Street special. I started to call my father Cruddums. The name stuck: he is now Cruddums to his grandchildren. During the workweek, Cruddums drove an hour into downtown Ottawa, where he'd spend the day sitting at his desk being a lawyer. When he returned home, he'd change into old blue work pants and steel-toed boots. A smelly, well-used cap finished the look—he'd become a farmer.

The farm's "lawns" had been hayfields when they bought the property; my mother mowed and mowed the areas close to the house. Eventually they were transformed into lawns. A neophyte gardener, she learned quickly, developing abundant flower beds and growing vegetables so that she could fill the freezer for the winter months.

My parents were organic farmers before their time. They kept cows; a steer was destined for the freezer each year. They gave the cattle only vaccinations, no growth hormones and no steroids. The vegetables in my mother's enormous garden were not sprayed with any kind of insecticide. She spent hours freezing green beans and many other kinds of produce for the winter months.

1970-1980

When I was 7, like many girls of that age, I wanted a pony. Since I'd never even sat on a horse, my parents thought it best if I had some lessons first. They contacted Spiritwood Farm in North Gower, Ontario, a 15-minute drive from our home in Burritts Rapids. I was, of course, incredibly excited.

Wearing work boots and a pair of faded jeans decorated with evidence of life on the farm, a woman called Joanna led Jasper, a small grey pony with an exuberant mane, into the sand ring at her farm. Jasper's naughty eyes peeked out from under his forelock, which was somewhat corralled between his ears. Someone had cut it straight across so that he could see.

The hard hat Mom had borrowed for the occasion was kept in place with an elastic strap under my chin. My hair, lacking much in terms of neatness and structure, was in pigtails that protruded boldly from beneath the hat. Mom had picked up the hard hat a couple of days ago; since then I'd been parading it proudly around the house. The "work boots" I was wearing had a heel that would stop my feet from slipping through the stirrups.

"Up you go," Joanna instructed. Jasper stood patiently; he was obviously used to beginner lessons. Joanna easily lifted me in the air. When I was suspended over Jasper, she lowered me softly onto the saddle.

"Let me show you how to hold the reins. Get used to how they feel in your hands. For the next couple of weeks, I'll lead you around, so that you'll become comfortable with the sensation of a pony moving underneath you. We'll do exercises. You'll soon relax so that you'll move in rhythm with Jasper. You won't even realize you're doing it."

I'd never been on a horse before, and when, after 20 minutes, the lesson was over, I wasn't ready for it to end. I would have liked it to go on. Forever.

The next summer, my parents—who I'm sure couldn't bear me in between the weekly lessons—bought me a pony. They figured that buying a pony, which they could keep on their farm, would be more economical than if I took more than one lesson a week. Cricket, a 14-hand bay pony with twinkling brown eyes and a thick black mane, was kind and easy for me to handle in the stable, but she was not nice to ride. When I rode her in the pasture next to the barn, she always ran back to the gate from the farthest reaches of the field. At the young age of 8, I didn't yet have the skills to correct her naughtiness. But I didn't give up, an early sign of the resilience that, as I got older, I had to frequently call upon.

When my parents told me that I could take my pony to the local fair, five miles down the road in Merrickville, I couldn't believe it. As far as I was concerned, it was a huge competition, fame awaiting the class winners.

Cricket and me, 1971.
Credit: Renée Smith

The day of the fair, my mind was crowded with dreams of upcoming glory when, having not slept a wink, I was out of bed before the alarm went off. The screen door of the barn scraped loudly along the concrete pad outside as I pulled it open, waking up Cricket, the cows and probably my parents sleeping in the house as well.

When the neighbour who would be trailering Cricket arrived, we loaded her with some difficulty, as she had almost never been in a trailer, and we drove to the fair. The butterflies in my stomach became more and more agitated as I nervously waited for our class, Beginner Equitation, to be called. The class would be judged on the rider's position in the saddle at the walk, trot and canter. At long last we entered the ring. Cricket and I were the only ones in the class, but the judge placed me first anyway. I got the red ribbon! Someone had told me that the judge would place me according to where she thought Cricket and I were ranked. I was delighted, sure that I was destined to be a superstar.

For the costume class, I dressed in a Santa Claus outfit. Cricket was the reindeer; we tied branches to her bridle so they looked like antlers growing from her head. We were, once again, the only competitors. Cricket's antlers slipped sideways, refusing to stay erect. Eventually I gave up holding them in place; they pointed horizontally at the few spectators leaning on the rail. Despite Cricket's collapsing costume, we again won the red ribbon.

The judge, Betty Cooper, had placed me first in both classes. To my mind, that was all that counted.

Daisy, a matronly chestnut mare of indeterminate breeding, came into my life in 1974. Goodhearted and kind, she was the perfect mount for an 11-year-old who had grown so tall for her age that she needed a horse rather than a pony. I rode her for three years. Then, in April 1977, when I was in Grade 10, a woman who ran a large stable in the area phoned my mother to tell her about a horse that had come into their barn and was for sale.

"You really should come and try him. Alder's only 4, but he seems to be very quiet. He's a lovely mover, and he jumps very safely. I think he'd make a great next horse for Claire." Alder was a quiet grey with Thoroughbred and Appaloosa blood. When I tried him, he seemed to suit. He was exactly the type, calibre and disposition that I was ready for. At that time, high school in Ontario included Grade 13 so, when Mom and Dad bought him, I'm sure they thought that Alder would do me for four years, at which time I'd stop riding because I'd be heading off to university.

When I got Alder, I started eventing. Horse trials (or events) have three phases, all of which must be completed by the same horse-and-rider combinations. At an event, the aim of the first phase, dressage, is to show that a horse who is in top physical form for the cross-country phase can perform a graceful, relaxed and precise test. It is sometimes difficult for riders to produce such a test with a horse who is fit enough to gallop and jump on the cross-country course.

At the lower levels of competition, dressage rings are 20 meters wide by 40 meters long. They are 20 by 60 meters at the international level. Alphabetic letters—the same letters are used around the world—mark positions around the outside of every dressage ring. When there is only one judge at the lower levels, this judge (who is always accompanied by a scribe) is positioned right behind the letter C. This is midway along the short side of the ring, opposite to the letter A, where the horses enter the ring. A dressage test consists of a pattern of movements that use the letters of the ring to indicate where movements begin or end. All horse-and-rider combinations competing at a certain level at an event, or in the same class at a dressage show, perform the same test. Alder was elegant and a beautiful mover, so we usually produced an outstanding dressage test.

For the cross-country phase, the second phase of a horse trial, the same horse-and-rider combinations complete a course of 15 to 40 solid natural obstacles that can't be lowered. A cross-country course features jumps that are cleverly designed to test the horses' fitness, accuracy, boldness and athleticism. These obstacles include banks, ditches and water. The goal is to complete this phase jumping cleanly, without incurring penalties for refusals or falls. Riders must complete the course under an optimum time. Penalties are accrued for each second over the time. At the lowest level, the level at which Alder and I started competing, the courses are only 2,000 meters in length. At the international level, they are over 6,000 meters long.

To prepare for the cross-country challenge at the lower levels, competitors walk the course just a couple of times. However, at the upper levels the courses are more difficult, so competitors walk the course several times during the days preceding the competition. Once on course, riders ready their horses, who are seeing the course for the first time, for each obstacle they face. They do so by adjusting the horse's speed and stride length.

The cross-country is followed by show jumping. This time, the same horse-and-rider combinations compete over a course of eight to twelve colourful jumps whose rails may fall if knocked by the horse. The object of this test is to jump cleanly, without lowering any rails, within an optimum time. The jumping test rewards fitness, the assumption being that a horse who is tired after the cross-country phase will have difficulty jumping a clear round. The jumping test is usually held in an arena or an enclosed space.

As the levels progress, the dressage test movements require a higher level of training, and the cross-country and jumping phases are longer and consist of more technically demanding jumps. Because the speed at which both the cross-country and jumping phases are ridden increases, the margin of error becomes smaller. At the international level, some jumps on the cross-country course can be as narrow as five feet across. Several obstacles of both the cross-country and jumping phases have multiple jumping efforts that are separated by very few strides.

James, a neighbour who had formerly ridden professionally, started to coach me. Originally from England, he had come to Canada to be the trainer at a local stable, which was where I'd met him a few years earlier. He'd married a Canadian after being in the country for a couple of years, and it was the incentive he'd needed to seek a more stable and permanent career. Articulate and well mannered, James was then just starting out in the real-estate business. Not all that long before he began to help me, he'd worked and lived a life with horses full time. By helping me, he could keep one foot in the horse world.

After successful seasons of eventing locally during the summers of 1977 to 1980, Alder and I moved up a level the next summer so that I could compete in the selection trials for the Ontario Junior Team, the team that would compete at the North American Championships in the sport of eventing. At that time, these championships were held yearly for dressage, jumping and eventing competitors under the age of 18. James, my mother and I drove the approximately six hours to Toronto every couple of weeks, always getting to the site the night before. The organizers tried to find stabling for Alder close by the competition; we were usually the only ones coming from any distance. We shared a room at a "horse-show motel." These were the cheapest motels that we could find located close to the stabling. After all, we only ever spent a short night—a few hours—in the room.

For one of the competitions, my father came along instead of my mother. Cruddums had always been supportive of my riding but had not been directly involved. The competition was in Collingwood, an almost eight-hour drive away. It was the farthest away of all the trials.

"Did we really need to leave at five a.m.?" my father, the "guest of honour," grumbled from his cramped position in the centre of the bench seat of the truck. A successful lawyer, he'd grown accustomed to a certain standard of comfort during his work day. Now he sat squished and hunching awkwardly, the middle one in a row of three. Always critical of the lack of support that car or truck bench seats offered, he'd arranged several rolled-up newspapers and various orthopedic supports behind and underneath him on the seat. None of us had much room, but James and I were used to it. Cruddums was not.

"Yes. We had to leave that early. I need to ride and walk the course when I get there." Nothing, not even a reluctant father, would soften me.

Cruddums also didn't understand our quick stops at service centres when we filled the truck with gas and checked on Alder.

"What is the hurry? Let me stretch!" He unfolded himself carefully and then creaked slowly out of the cramped space. His strategically placed seat supports flew freely around the cab and out the opened door.

I lunged for a bundle of newspapers that was held tightly in a roll with masking tape, managing to grab it before it landed in the puddle just outside the passenger door.

Service centres tend to have dirty washrooms and terrible coffee. James and I just wanted to get to where we were going, so we were quickly on the road again. Although we were used to gas station coffee, Dad was not, and he found the cheap coffee we bought unbearable. He removed the plastic lid from the Styrofoam cup as we made our way along the highway and asked me to pour the watery mass out the window, as he was unable to do so from his jammed position in the centre.

Several hours later, after making sure that Alder was set up for the evening, we drove to the motel I'd chosen because it was closest to Alder's stabling. After inspecting the bathroom, my father emerged holding a threadbare towel at arm's length.

"Is this the best they can do?" His shoulders drooped; it was even worse that he expected.

"Well, I think this place is great. It's close to the event and the stabling." My enthusiastic reply was received by an extremely grumpy face. I now know that my father was wondering whether evidence of his careful upbringing would ever show up in his daughter.

Alder's dressage was so good, thanks to James's coaching, that we won two out of the four Ontario junior team trials and placed third in the other two. To everyone's complete surprise, we were the top qualifiers, so we were chosen for the team. I hadn't expected to be successful that first year, so I was, of course, elated. After that, Alder and I went to a weeklong training camp near Toronto.

The whole training camp experience felt very foreign. I was taken away from James, my regular coach. Of course, I didn't recognize that, at age 17, I would never be a team player. I certainly hadn't yet realized that, in any team situation, there would be times when I would have to "play the game," even though it might not have been how I normally did things. But I soon found out that my little world, the one I had created, the one that had always worked for me, was no longer available. I had to adapt my system to the situation in which I found myself at the training camp for the Ontario team.

I do know that I wasn't at all sure of the coach. Although he had years of experience, he didn't know me and wasn't familiar with Alder. Alder had always won dressage, but the new coach changed his outline so that his frame—the shape of his body—was incorrect. Naturally, horses carry a lot of their body weight on their front legs. Dressage tips their bodies so that they carry more of their weight on their hind legs and become more balanced. But after the training camp, Alder's hindquarters no longer assumed their portion of his body weight.

James, who hadn't worked with Alder and me since before the camp, flew out to Alberta, where the junior championships were being held, in order to coach me. James did his best to try to fix the problem, but when it was our turn to do the dressage test a couple of days later, the test was far below the quality we usually produced. Our score wasn't good either; we were heavily penalized for Alder's incorrect frame. Alder and I, completely uncharacteristically, finished near the bottom of the dressage. We completed the cross-country and the jumping, but Alder refused twice on cross-country, which was completely unlike him. Although we finished the competition, I was shattered and distraught, disillusioned by the whole team experience.

The North American junior championships in Alberta were my first experience competing as a member of a team. The training camp and the competition that followed left a bitter taste in my mouth that did not go away at subsequent competitions while I was a member of a team. Over the years, although each team situation was different, I was never comfortable and I never felt ready to perform at my best in any environment when my control was taken away.

If I couldn't be in control of my own routine, and my comfortable, self-created, regular support system was removed or changed, I felt rudderless. I completely fell apart. If I was not the captain in charge of my own ship, I never learned how to cope. When I could manage and supervise my familiar group of supporters, I could do the job well, even when I was in unfamiliar territory.

In any team situation, one is expected to "go with the flow"; however, I didn't easily adapt to change. Although I'm still super organized and very detail-oriented, during the time I was competing my horses, I never understood that some people aren't either of these things, and that it's okay. It works for them. But because it was completely unfamiliar to my way of doing things, I found it impossible to let it slide, to understand that it didn't matter. I never accepted that while I did my own thing, they could do theirs.

Over the years, I've changed. Only when team riding was long in my past did I realize that the way in which others run their lives is beyond my control. No longer obsessing over small details, I now try to focus on the bigger picture. I'm finally able to open my eyes to the fact that throughout life many situations are not ideal; things are not always the way we want them to be. I've learned that the world is not perfect and that I can't let it bother me—otherwise, I would drive myself crazy. However, at the time it didn't occur to me to just let go of the things that weren't under my control.

Tunnel Vision

1981–1997

The horse-crazed young girl I was became an obsessive teenager, who evolved into an over-motivated young adult. I spent hours in the barn and yet more hours training and riding my horses. On the Saturday night of my high-school prom, I was in Toronto competing in one of the selection trials for the eventing team that would represent Ontario at the North American junior championships. I didn't even consider missing the trial and going to the prom instead.

I'm not sure when I crossed the line between hobby and obsession, but it soon became clear to everyone around me that the itch that had started when I was young was just not going to go away. I had a singular identity: I was a rider. I had no desire to explore other interests, no curiosity about any other facets of my self, no interest in discovering who I might also be. My world had one dimension: equestrian sport.

There was something else feeding my desire, although I did not recognize it until much later. Fuelling my inner drive was a need that's a basic part of who I am: I'm someone who's always working toward a goal. Although a more traditional goal might have produced stability and an income, the only thing I wanted to do was ride. It was never a conscious decision, but at some point during my teenage years my goal became reaching for the top of my sport. I worked relentlessly hard at achieving that goal.

In September 1981, feeling completely crushed after my first team experience, I became a student at Queen's University. During the four years that I was there, I worked toward a Bachelor of Science degree. While I was at university, I kept a horse at a local farm just outside Kingston so that I could keep my finger in the equestrian pie. My undergraduate years at Queen's University suited me to a T, providing me with a degree with which I'd be able to partially fund my passion.

When I graduated from the four-year undergraduate program in computer science in 1985, I was ready to begin the next stage of my life. But what would that next stage be? My parents assumed that I would seek employment in the field of computer science. But would that be my calling? Would I spend the employable years of my life pursuing that career? I wasn't so sure. As far as I was concerned, the time I'd spent at Queen's University had only been a detour that my parents had made me take.

My sole interest was pursuing the equestrian dream. Fortunately, considering my equestrian aspirations, the BSc in computer science proved to be useful: it gave me the skills necessary to work as a computer programmer for the federal government on a contract basis. The first contract started in the fall of 1985, and I kept signing them. Initially they were for 12 months and then, beginning in 1991, I had one for every May to December until December 1994. My horses stayed on my parents' farm. Commuting into Ottawa at six in the morning, I could be back at four in the afternoon to ride my horses. I was up at five every morning, only crashing back into bed at ten at night. In retrospect, I see clearly that those were crazy days. However, at the time I wasn't bothered by my schedule. I just kept working away at my dream of riding at the international level.

During the winter months of those years, I often braved the inhospitable conditions to go to indoor schooling shows. Indoor arenas provide a small, refrigerator-like space that is at least free of snow and has soft footing for the horses. Although these arenas enable some training during the seemingly endless winter months, the space is small. This makes it impossible to develop a horse's fitness, which is essential for competing at the upper levels.

Early one Saturday morning in January 1990, the alarm jangled loudly on the table next to my bed. At 6 a.m., it was still pitch black outside. Even though I dressed in so many layers that I'd become almost blob-like, when I unlocked the mudroom door to head out to the barn, the winter hit me full on. The freezing air quickly sucked the excitement I had felt about going to the competition right out of me.

Waddling through the darkness to the barn, I readied Patrick, a horse I'd bought a couple of years earlier, bandaging his lower legs for protection just before I loaded him in the trailer. When I stopped by the house on my way out, my mother emerged from the mudroom holding two cups of coffee. She slid into the passenger seat.

"Are you sure you want to go?" she asked. Shivering, she clutched a coffee in each hand. I was envious of those hands, each wrapped around a warm coffee. I was cold all over, having spent the last hour in an unheated barn.

"Claire, when did you start the truck? It's absolutely freezing." I was irritated at my mother's remark. She'd just come out of a warm house!

It was years before the invention of heated seats. "Mom, I started the truck 10 minutes ago. It'll be warm soon." I needed to remember she was doing me a huge favour by coming along to help.

We got to the show, unloaded Patrick and tacked him up. Because the indoor space at the competition was very limited, warm-up—preparing for a class—was done in a group. Before each class started, the riders had 10 minutes in the indoor ring to loosen up their horses on the flat before jumping a few fences. I led Patrick into the ring and mounted.

There were only three minutes left in my warm-up time when Patrick and I jumped a couple of times. We left the ring and then stood around waiting until the start of our class. The warm-up had been far from adequate, but it was the best possible in a frigid Canadian January. All the riders had heaped blankets over their horses to keep their muscles warm. They shrugged ski jackets over their shoulders and pulled winter mitts over their gloves.

Welcome to a Canadian winter.

After spending a few winters at home in Canada, it became apparent that I had to make a change if I wanted to continue to improve, and if I wanted to satisfy my desire to compete at the higher levels with some chance of success. In the southern States, I could get started with training and fitness work in January instead of spending the winter months in an indoor arena. The level and calibre of horses, riders and coaches in the horse community at home in eastern Canada was limiting. I needed to spread my wings so that I could observe and listen to riders from farther afield. Going to an area where I could train more seriously under the guidance of coaches with huge CVs would be invaluable. On a more traditional adventure, like a long trip to Europe after university, individuals experience wider, more varied cultures than they would if they stayed in Canada. Similarly, I would be exposed to a much larger world than the small network in which I had grown up.

In January 1991, Lorraine, a local coach who'd ridden on the national team, was planning a trip to Southern Pines, North Carolina. She would be taking several of her students south, setting up training programs for them and going to the spring competitions. I had a couple of horses to train and compete. Master Sing, a bay gelding sired by an English stallion who was much sought after in the sport, had come into my life the previous summer. Patrick was a horse I'd owned for the last couple of years. I knew, however, that Patrick wasn't of the calibre necessary to compete at the level to which I aspired.

Pinehurst, a golf destination for many, is only 10 minutes away from where our horses were stabled. Around the many golf courses there is a plethora of townhouses to rent. I shared one with two other girls who were riding with Lorraine. We were all in our early twenties, our "grownup" lives just starting—but we had a long way to go before reaching that stage. There were many late nights, lots of bottles of alcohol and always extra people in our condominium. Housekeeping was a foreign word. I still remember that once when Lorraine was visiting she came out of the bathroom, half laughing and half crying.

"Girls, when you trim your toenails, put the clippings in the wastepaper basket. There are bits all over the floor!"

My elbows rested on the railing of the show ring next to the stable we'd rented. The informal horse show that was in progress was one of the many that were held regularly in Southern Pines, both on the weekends and during the week. It was warm even for March, so I'd stripped off my sweatshirt; the green tank top and bright yellow sports bra underneath it exposed my shoulders to the sun. The region's prolific rhododendrons had already come out; vivid swatches of pink and purple were liberally sprinkled over the landscape.

A young man I'd seen riding on the trails with one of the local trainers came over and leaned on the railing next to me.

"Are you on a break from working for the trainer?" I asked.

He looked surprised. "Oh, I don't work for him," he told me. "I just like the experience of riding other horses. I have one of my own, but I only ride for fun. I'm a doctor in the next town. Harry." He did look like a stereotypical doctor. About my height, he was thin and had a slightly receding hairline. He looked at me through wire-rimmed glasses. As soon as Harry said he was a doctor, my curiosity was immediately piqued: I wanted to find out whether he was single. In retrospect, I'll admit that my interest was very superficial.

I asked, "So is your wife here watching the show with you? Is she interested in horses?"

"I'm divorced. Are you one of the Canadian girls here for the winter? Have you seen the coast of North Carolina? Any other parts of it? Southern Pines is such an anomaly in the state," Harry told me.

"Yes, I'm Canadian—down for a few months. No, I haven't seen anything but Southern Pines and Pinehurst."

Harry had an airplane and offered to fly me to the coast—where he had a condominium—for dinner the next night. *Yes, yes, yes!* Harry took me east in his plane. I'd never flown in a small plane before, so I found the experience a little nerve-wracking. During the flight, I found out more about him, including that he was almost 40, a whole 14 years older than I was. *Yikes,* I thought, but it didn't deter me.

Harry and I started spending more time together. It was perfect, really. I was committed to my horses and Harry to his job, his airplane and the gym. During the week, he had a never-changing routine—work, gym, same take-out dinner most nights—and so he was busy until later in the evenings. In town only during the early-winter months, I was intently focused on my horses. Although I was riding seven days a week, we occasionally flew to his condominium on the coast of North Carolina on a Friday for an overnight stay. I think that he was relieved to find someone who fit so nicely and conveniently into his life.

It's amazing that we continued in this way for several years. Content living our own lives, we didn't threaten each other's worlds or plan for any future beyond each weekend. After I travelled home to Canada in May, Harry flew his airplane up a couple of times each summer to stay for the weekend. That was enough for me because my free time was so limited. I was at work in Ottawa at 7 a.m. Then, when I got home at 4 p.m., I rode until dark. I was concerned only with my horses. Harry was such a creature of habit and routine that our relationship suited him too—he could just carry on the way he'd always been. Few emotional demands were made of either of us. Being together, however one might interpret that phrase, didn't disrupt our lives.

In February 1992, I was once again in North Carolina for a few winter months. I owned Master Sing, who was super talented but also very prone to injury. I needed to find a young prospect with a little experience and enough talent to make it to the top. I increasingly focused on following my dream; it teased the tip of my being. I kept working and striving. I realized that my parents were willing to finance my efforts, but only while they saw how hard I worked. They made it possible for me to follow my dreams. Had I at any point along the journey taken their support for granted, it would have been quickly withdrawn.

At the time I was competing, it was much easier to buy a talented young horse with some experience in England than it was to find one at home. There were so many more horses available there. They had many competitions, and the sport was exceptionally popular. I left my barn in Southern Pines one afternoon to drive to Raleigh, where I caught a plane to Atlanta, Georgia. I carried my video camera and a small suitcase containing my riding clothes, a pair of pajamas, and not a whole lot else, except rain gear and sweaters. The weather in England in January is raw, cold and rainy. It is, in fact, like the weather I was leaving behind in North Carolina.

When the plane landed in London early the next morning, I was desperately in need of a shower and a cozy, warm bed into which I could collapse. But this was not a holiday. When I finally dragged my jet-lagged, exhausted self out of the warm, claustrophobic plane and into Heathrow airport, I met Sue (the agent from Canada who had sourced the horses I was to try) at the baggage claim.

It was only nine in the morning when I drove from the airport with Sue—on the left-hand side of the road—and soon disappeared into the soggy English winter.

"We've got three to see today," Sue told me. "But stop as soon as you can. We need coffee."

After about an hour's drive, we pulled into a farm in Hampshire. There, in a raw, damp unheated room typical of houses in England, I peeled off my laundry-worthy airplane clothes. Shivering, I opened my suitcase and found the many layers I had packed. Sweaters. Raincoats. Warm gloves. Breeches.

Sue and her contact in England thought that Gordon Gibbons was the best match in terms of what I needed, so they had arranged for me to try him right away. A six-year-old bay gelding, he jumped very well, tucking his knees up safely. He had oodles of scope—nothing was an effort—and an enormous gallop stride. His walk and trot were good but not exceptional. I could imagine him producing a workman-like, correct dressage test but never a flashy one. By riding Gordon first, I allowed myself a couple of days at the end of my short trip to try him again. Both times I thought he was great, an extraordinary athlete. The other horses I tried didn't make any lasting impression on me, so I flew back to North Carolina with my fingers crossed, hoping that Gordon would pass the prepurchase veterinary exam.

Such an exam consists of a series of tests to determine whether a horse has any conditions that may, over time, lead to lameness. The vet critically watches the horse walk, trot and canter and then stresses the joints of its legs. By watching the horse trot away each time stress is applied to a joint, the vet determines whether the stress causes unsoundness in the horse. If it does, it is an indication that there may be future problems in that joint, so the vet may choose to take several X-ray views of the area, in addition to the standard X-rays that are usually taken of the horse's limbs during the exam. These X-rays may confirm any suspicions the vet has after a visual exam of the horse's movement, because they allow the vet to see any abnormalities that might lead to future lameness. The vet also carefully tests for any irregularities in the horse's vision, breathing and musculature.

Gordon passed the prepurchase exam and was flown from England to New York. After a short, two-day quarantine, a horse transport company trailered him to Southern Pines, dropping him off late one night at the stable at which I'd rented stalls.

When I got there early the next morning, Gordon was spinning in his stall. Around and around he went, slowing down only occasionally to look out the window. His stall was in complete disarray, a mess of stirred-up bedding. I unlatched the stall door and waited in the doorway for him to calm down. He eventually slowed and stopped, then he cautiously sniffed my outreached hand, giving me permission to venture into his space.

Anxiety and fear filled Gordon's eyes, not the calm and trust that I'd expected to see. His long journey from the cargo airport in Upper New York State had ended very late the night before, and then he'd been put into an unfamiliar stall in a foreign barn. The whole ordeal spelled total confusion to him; he was panicked by his strange surroundings. Covered in sweat from his chaotic night, he looked drawn and dehydrated.

I spent many hours the first couple of days hand-walking Gordon, giving him lots of time to check out his surroundings. Then, when he was calmer, I turned him out in a paddock close to the barn. Although he was the only one in it, he was surrounded by horses in adjoining paddocks. When I turned him out, he usually was quiet and seemed content to draw comfort from the horses around him. I didn't yet realize that this deeply ingrained pack instinct was the initial hint of Gordon's insecurities.

One day, when I had yet to ride him, Gordon was turned out in a paddock when the local fox hunt came through the farm, its hounds and horses making their way between the farm's paddocks. In every fox hunt, the hounds are guided by the huntsman and a couple of whippers-in. They are followed by a field master who leads the field, the group of riders taking part in the hunt. The hunt traversed the property occasionally, so we were all used to it.

But when Gordon saw the hunt on the other side of his paddock fence, he slowly trotted up to the fence. It was about five feet high at that point, four two-by-eight planks topped by a rail. It seemed much higher, though, situated as it was at the top of an incline. Gordon neatly popped over it, still at a trot. I watched it all in total disbelief. My first thought was, *Wow—what an athlete!* My excitement was, however, immediately followed by the thought, *What do I do now?* To my immense relief, Gordon appeared to be afraid of the hunt, so he made his way over to another paddock and nuzzled the horse there. I was speechless, in total awe of this tremendous athlete who had come into my life.

My next problem was how to channel the talent and energy of this remarkable phenomenon. Once he had settled in, I started to ride Gordon. Unlike the calm horse he had appeared to be before I bought him, for the first few months that I had him he panicked whenever he was ridden. Very insecure, he would rear up on his hind legs and then spin around and head home. Great. I owned a spectacular athlete, but I couldn't ride him. Gordon dreaded any change in his life; every new routine was calamitous to him. Until I learned how to deal with his issues, he was a real pain.

I didn't have a clue how to deal with this athletic yet very insecure horse, so I called up Mike Plumb, who had a farm just five minutes away. An eight-time Olympian and Equestrian Hall of Fame member, Mike could figure out this horse if anyone could. When he arrived to ride Gordon, he was wearing a helmet, which was very unusual; at the time, few people did. I'll never forget watching as Mike rode Gordon the first time. Although I was a bit surprised that Gordon didn't panic or spin, I think that he sensed Mike's tremendous experience. Mike picked up a canter and jumped a small fence. He pulled up, looked over to me and said, "This horse is a Cadillac." For Mike, that was the highest of compliments. I settled into a training program with Mike.

During the summer months that followed, I again worked for the government on a contract basis. By living at home on my parent's farm, I could sock away all the money I made, saving it for my trips south in the winter. Mike spent his summers in an area north of Boston, at that time a hub for equestrian activity, so I trailered my horses down to Hamilton, Massachusetts, for a few days whenever I could.

Master Sing won the 1992 Canadian Championships that September. Gordon was a work in progress, offering me only glimpses of the tremendous athlete he was. However, although these moments kept me thinking that it was all worthwhile, they were sprinkled haphazardly between long periods of frustration on my part.

Master Sing competing at Rolex Kentucky Horse
Trials, Lexington, Kentucky, circa 1995.
Credit: VW Perry Photographic

Now

Annie lies stretched out on the pine floor of my office, soaking up the warmth of the April sun pouring in through the windows. I've finally realized that everyday pleasures—which can be as simple as watching my dog sleep—help make the present, the *Now*, as important and as relevant to me as my memories of the way life used to be.

Even though I'm finally happy in my own skin, enjoying my life *Now*, my past still has the power to stop me in my tracks. So, although I yearn to lie on the sofa in that same sun, devouring the final pages of the novel that I'm reading, I resist and stay at my desk because it's one of those times. I never know when my memories will surface, but it happens. Suddenly, I'll be flooded by words, thoughts and imaginings.

Memories of my past appear less and less frequently, so when they do interrupt my *Now*, I don't let them slither out of reach. Instead, I embrace the memories, capturing them and sculpting them into words. I'm all too aware that if I don't stop what I'm doing and pour words that describe those precious times into my computer, the memories will quickly slide back into my mind's depths and disappear.

When that happens, I'll just have to wait until the next time.

Southern Pines Vignettes

1993–1997

Everything started to come together in the early spring of 1993. After successful spring and fall competition seasons, Gordon and I were the highest-placed Canadians at the fall 1993 US Championships. Although they are the US Championships, they're open to riders from around the world. However, during those years, the competitors were usually North American. The spring of 1994 was again successful, so Gordon and I were chosen to be members of the Canadian team at the 1994 world championships.

From 1993 to 1997 Kim groomed for me. She'd been recommended by my friend Anne, who ran the equestrian program at a college near my home in Canada. Thorough, dedicated and a quick learner, Kim had the responsibility for the horses' care and well-being. I was incredibly lucky. She was so good at her job, and so conscientious, that I never had to worry about how the horses were being looked after. I could concentrate on riding.

Kim leading Gordon before the cross-country at the
1995 US Fall Championships. We placed 6th.
Credit: Renée Smith

I got an early start to the competition season by escaping the Canadian winter and spending most of January through until late April in Southern Pines. Every January my father listened anxiously to the in-depth, detailed weather reports broadcast over a special station to which he subscribed. I was packed up and all ready to go but ready to delay our departure when storms were forecast. They gathered speed across Lake Ontario and then hit the eastern shore of the lake between Watertown and Syracuse with a pounding fury. Driving, especially when one is pulling a large horse trailer, is no fun at all if there's lots of blowing snow off the lake.

On the first day that it seemed the weather would be calm, I crossed my fingers and prayed that the storms would stay away. Kim and I headed south on our journey to a climate more suited for training in the winter. I always did all the driving; I found that being in the passenger seat was not at all restful for me. The story of the yearly trip is one that remains etched in my memory.

Early one January day, before the sun was up, we left the awful weather behind. It was cold. As is typical that time of year in Ontario, there was a biting wind and lots of snow that mixed messily with my thoughts of the warmer climate of Southern Pines, where we were headed in North Carolina. Every January. Every year.

Kim, her long, curly mass of red hair tied back, led tall, anxious-eyed Gordon to the trailer. He bounded up the ramp and we backed him into a stall. Then, one by one, we loaded Master Sing and the other two or three horses that I was taking. The horses changed because I sold the ones that weren't working for me and occasionally bought other young prospects. Among others, Hubcap was one I'd owned for a couple of years. Although he was a spectacular jumper, he was basically lazy. Before he frustrated me completely, I sold him. One year there was Freddie. He was a horse that I'd taken a chance on when he was quite young and inexperienced, but in the end he hadn't amounted to much, so I'd sold him. Martin was another. Sometimes I'd be lucky enough to have one along that was being sent by its owner for training.

Hubcap was an amazing jumper. Millbrook
Horse Trails, circa 1995.
Credit: Terri Miller Photography

We climbed into the cab of the truck. After the diesel engine rumbled to life, I released the handbrake. We were off! Almost.

I could always predict what happened next. Each time I maneuvered my enormous trailer around the circular driveway, my father appeared at the back door of the house. He wanted us to stop so that he could lift the hood and check the oil. We always just waved goodbye and drove on.

The trip never varied much. We stopped at different diesel stations, but that was it. The service centres along the main highways accommodate semitrailers, so my rig (I thought it was huge, but it wasn't in comparison to the semis) could be easily maneuvered to get diesel. We knew which places had half-decent coffee for a service centre as well as clean restrooms. We took time on these stops to offer the horses water and to strip off, one by one, their layers of blankets; the weather was usually warmer the further south we went. We replenished our supply of junk food: chips, gummy bears and peanut butter and crackers. After 10 hours on the road, we always stopped for the night at a friend's farm in Pennsylvania. She had welcoming beds for us and stalls for the horses.

We were up early the following day and soon on our way. First we made our way along the congested toll roads circling Baltimore, then those around Washington and then endlessly south on many more monotonous four-lane highways. Not only did all the highways look the same, they really were the same. We listened to a lot of books on tape, but I found it hard to concentrate and make sense of them until after we had passed the big cities.

After nine more hours of driving, we finally arrived at our winter home. During the early winters of 1995 to 1997, I rented stalls in an old shed row hidden at the back of a farm that featured a new, more showy barn along the road. Bruce, who was sponsored by the lady who owned the farm, kept his horses in the new barn. After unloading our horses, we hung water buckets for them and threw lots of hay over the half doors onto the floors of the stalls.

"Good night, boys. See you in the morning." At long last we got to go to bed.

I certainly don't miss the 8:30 a.m. start to my day at the barn during those years that I wintered in North Carolina.

People think of North Carolina as sunny and warm, but its Januarys and Februarys are not at all warm. They are cold and raw. Biting. The damp air seeps in through layered clothing and wraps itself tightly around, the cold invading and holding your body hostage. It didn't seem to matter what clothing I wore during those years of focus, of grit, of determination. Gloves got wet all the time from cleaning buckets and washing horses. Fingers became wrinkled from the constant exposure to water; then it seemed that in no time they were chapped. Hand cream and Vaseline under gloves only helped so much. The sandy soil mixed with the grease to create an unbearable scratchy, painful potion held in place by the gloves. It was worth it, though, because in this area the ground was almost always thawed by late morning, so the horses could be ridden on the soft footing. People flooded to the area with their horses after Christmas, seeking sanctuary from the frozen, snow-covered north, and they stayed for the winter months.

During those months of reprieve from snowy Canada, I ran almost every morning. The days started silently. I quietly crawled out of bed at 6 a.m. Tiptoeing into the bathroom, I washed my face, brushed my teeth, dressed in running clothes and then felt my way through the dark without turning on any lights. The door creaked closed behind me as I crept out of the silent house, leaving the family I boarded with soundly asleep. The diesel engine in my enormous truck made a lot of noise. I cringed as it started, released the parking brake and eased out the driveway. I drove four miles to the gym. Once there, I chose a treadmill facing a TV tuned to the morning news. Multi-tasking, I ran five miles while learning what was new in the world. After a quick shower, I changed into my riding clothes and then drove to the barn via the coffee shop, where I always ordered two black coffees and a toasted cinnamon-raisin bagel, no butter.

My truck knew the way, seeming to turn left automatically into the driveway of my coach and friend, Mike.

"Mike! Good morning!" I handed him a coffee wherever he was, which was usually sitting atop a horse, about to head into the ring.

At the next farm, I turned off the road again, my diesel truck rumbling up the driveway, heading toward the old shed-row barn at the back of the property. Kim had been there for at least an hour, and the horses had been fed. This was a typical February morning in Southern Pines—it was cold.

"Good morning!" I never heard much, just muttering coming from Gordon's stall. Kim was not a morning person.

"I'll take Hubcap out for his grass, so about 20 minutes?" I never got an answer.

During the early months of 1997, I would hand-graze Hubcap when I arrived at the barn after running at the gym. He was on stall rest because of an injury, only allowed out for short sessions twice a day. There were just glimpses of the coming day. The end of the long lead line stuffed into my pocket along with my freezing fingers, I had nothing to do but watch the emerging sun slowly begin to crack through the cold, the frosty landscape gradually softening as the sun rose. I tried to enjoy the peaceful interlude as much as the cold would allow me to, attempting to interpret the sky as it hinted at the weather of the coming day. It was so damp, raw and cold those mornings that I always found myself counting down the minutes until I could take my horse back to his stall.

When Hubcap and I got back to the barn, Kim had Gordon tacked up and waiting for me.

"Thanks, Kim. I'll ride Freddie after Gord."

Inevitably, a biting wind snuck in under my clothes and, searching for my bare skin, curled its way up my back as Gordon crunched through the frozen sand of the driveway. Before the raw air made it all the way in, I snugged up the cord that tightened my ski jacket's waistband and buried my chin into the turtleneck I was wearing. The turtleneck was covered by the thin windbreaker that I always wore at that time of year. Then came my blue polar-fleece sweater, and lastly my ski jacket. I'd made myself as warm and windproof as I could, but the mean cold wind would still manage to make its presence felt.

Reaching the end of the driveway, Gordon and I clattered across the paved road and then slipped through a narrow opening in the fence line along the other side. We were now in the Foundation, a 5,000-acre wooded area with trails to which the horse community was lucky to have unlimited access.

A horse and rider made their way along the path toward us.

"Hey, Marc. A little chilly today." I put both reins into my frozen left hand and then shoved the numb fingers of my right hand into my pocket.

"You got it! How's Gordon?" Marc asked. "He looks ready for something!" There were four or five competitions before the spring championships in Lexington, Kentucky. The first one was in Altoona, Florida.

"I'm going down for the trials in February. I've got a bit of time, although Gordon seems to be waiting for the competitions to start!" Gordon had only been standing for 10 seconds, but he was fidgety and started to walk off.

"I guess we're leaving! Dinner tonight?" Marc nodded, so we quickly planned to meet at a local restaurant.

After a walk of a half an hour or so, Gord and I slipped through the opening in the fence line and crossed the road. I rode over to the dressage ring behind my barn, where I met Mike for a lesson.

Mike and I had an arrangement whereby I paid him a monthly fee. Some days he had time for four horses, but more often it was just for one or two. But this just meant that he didn't have the time to focus only on me and on the horse I was riding. Several times a day, I slipped through the opening in the fence behind my barn that led to Mike's farm, and I worked one of my horses while he was riding one of his. I occasionally heard comments, criticisms or suggestions directed at me. But no matter how late he was or how many horses he still had to ride, Mike almost always made time in his day to focus on Gordon. It was a rare occasion when the day was too short and he had no time for us.

The old picnic table at C, where a judge would be seated, wobbled a little when Mike hopped up to sit on top of it, his feet on its seat.

"How's Gordon today? And when is Bruce going to replace this picnic table? It's not long for this world."

Mike watched Gordon and me intently as I practised the movements for our upcoming dressage test—but not in the same order as they appeared in the test. Creatures of habit, horses thrive on routine. They don't know enough, however, not to learn a test and anticipate what's going to happen next. Gordon's dressage was solid and dependable—very accurate, it was correct and workman-like. He was not an expressive mover. His walk, trot and canter were average, not flashy at all. At the time when I was competing, there were few event horses that were showy in the dressage phase. The most important quality for eventing is the same now as it was then: the horses must gallop well and jump safely.

Although Mike sat silently, the black baseball hat and dark sunglasses that he always wore hid eyes that carefully watched our every move. "Make a more definite transition from trot to canter. Make it accurate, right on the letter … Good…Better."

"Work on the 10-meter circle into half pass." Gordon and I were cantering. Bang at the letter B, we smoothly transitioned to an active working trot.

"Good transition."

I rode up to A and turned down the centre line. When I got to X, I began to ride a 10-meter circle to the right, toward the letter B. Mike's dark glasses followed every step.

"I think you need more bend in his neck." I continued the circle, more mindful after listening to Mike that Gordon was bent throughout his body to the same degree as the circle.

"That's better. Now keep him bent during the half pass. He tends to be too straight in his neck in the right half pass."

After just 20 minutes, we were done. Gordon knew his stuff. With Mike's help, I just needed to tune him, to practise without him becoming bored. I dropped my reins so Gord could stretch his neck. His whole body relaxed.

"Thanks, Mike. I'll ride Freddie over in a bit."

That Wednesday, the forecast was for freezing rain. Tuesday evening, like any night before bad weather arrived, the supermarkets were packed with people. The milk, eggs and bread quickly sold out.

The first time they called for bad weather, I snickered to myself, thinking of all the experience I had because I came from Ontario. It was funny to see everyone overreact. I thought I would be fine because I was so used to icy winter conditions in Canada. However, winter driving can be much more treacherous in North Carolina than in Canada because they don't have salt and sand at the ready, but I was always convinced that I could handle it. Over the years, although perhaps I should have done so, I never learned—or accepted—that things were different this far south. Here they were ill prepared for any snow, ice or freezing rain.

Early the next morning, when I got into my truck to drive to the gym, the gravel on the driveway was coated with ice. Because it was bumpy, it wasn't slippery at all. However, when I turned onto the paved road, I immediately started to slide off, heading quickly toward the ditch. I'd forgotten, again, that there are no salt trucks in North Carolina—no sand, nothing. It is lethal on the roads after a freeze! It didn't seem to matter that I'd spent years at home driving in conditions that were far worse. In Canada, there are snowploughs and salt trucks that are called into action when there is the slightest chance of snow, so the roads are clear—and safe. I gave up on my morning run; the truck and I crawled back to the house.

At 7 a.m., I phoned Kim. It rang and rang. Kim is not a morning person. Finally she picked up.

"Morning, Kim!" Kim mumbled something in reply.

"The roads are awful, so let's delay going to the barn for an hour. The horses will be fine."

I sensed through the phone line that Kim was thrilled at the prospect of going back to bed for a bit.

"I'll call you in an hour, and we'll decide who will venture out to the barn."

The town was quiet that morning, but the morning's enforced hibernation didn't last long. By mid-afternoon, the ice had all melted. The bread was put in the freezer for the next time. The eggs and milk lasted me for the week.

When the long day ended at about six o'clock during those damp winter months in North Carolina, I spent ages in the shower, shivering while I slowly thawed out. Clean and warm at last, my cozy sheepskin slippers hugging my feet, I headed into the living room and put the day's video into the VCR. Every evening I watched the videos that Kim had taken that day. There was always one of me riding Gordon and often one of me riding one or two of the other horses as well.

Although it would have been easier to stay on the couch, after a while I usually did get up. Pulling on a clean pair of jeans, I would head to a local restaurant to meet other riders. Even though it was still early, we were usually famished after our days with our horses. Dinner was often our only real food of the day. A lot of us subsisted on snacks bought in haste at the local convenience store until dinnertime rolled around.

We were impatient and hungry, ordering quickly after only glancing at the menu, which we usually knew by heart anyway. When the food came, we ate it all. Satiated, we would be sleepy by then but would sit around and chat while we finished our beers.

After leaving the restaurant, I would drive to the barn, only about 10 minutes away, to do night check. Rather than asking Kim to go back to the barn, I enjoyed this time alone with my horses. Kim had already had a long day and deserved not to have to go out again. At nine o'clock, it was quiet and dark. Peaceful.

My main man, Gordon, always wove back and forth at the thought of food. Leaning dangerously far over the half door of his stall, he stretched himself into the aisle. He then wildly circled, shavings scattering throughout his stall, some landing in his water buckets. Tidying up his bed after that evening performance was part of my routine.

A couple of stalls further along, Sing's bright and naughty eyes caught mine as he, too, leaned into the aisle. He danced silently, waving his right foot in the air, pawing quietly for food.

Just a minute, boys.

There were usually five geldings in the barn. I fed them their individually prepared gourmet dinners. As they delighted noisily in the grain, I did the other night-check duties: hay, water, muck out the stalls, change blankets.

Goodnight, boys.

Checking the stall doors when I finished, I made sure each was fastened. In the truck once more, I made my way back to the house where I rented a room. I didn't think too long before deciding that my laundry could wait until the next day. Collapsing into bed, I fell asleep—immediately.

The time spent in Southern Pines each winter made a big difference to me. As well as being able to prepare properly for the spring trials, I could focus just on my horses. Even after I'd stopped doing computer work and spent my whole day in the barn, I still felt scattered when I was in Canada. There always seemed to be things to do that had nothing to do with my riding, so I was less able to direct my energies solely in the direction of my horses.

Gordon jumping into the water at Fair Hill United States
Fall Championships, 1995. We finished in 6th place.
Credit: Terri Miller Photography

Credit: Terri Miller Photography

The Atlanta Olympics

- -

Kim, Gordon and I worked relentlessly long hours throughout the tension-filled early-spring months of 1996, during which the selection trials were held to choose the team to represent Canada at the Olympics in Atlanta, Georgia. The trials culminated with the spring championships at Kentucky in April. I was ecstatic when we were chosen to be part of the Canadian team. Gordon had always received five-star treatment that catered to his every need, and I was forever careful about his health and soundness. That spring, however, our concern for Gordon's welfare reached the point of paranoia, with the result that we were anxious all the time, watching poor Gord's every move and treating him as if he were gold.

Once a horse-and-rider combination was chosen for the team, a large part of the preparation involved acclimatizing to the oppressive heat in Atlanta at the end of July. We went to a training camp near Atlanta for the two weeks just before the Games. Only an hour or two from the Olympic venue, the entire Canadian Equestrian Team was there. The jumper riders and the dressage riders shared the facility with the three-day event riders.

During this period, all the athletes were drug-tested. Although there are no drugs that would help an equestrian athlete, they also checked for illicit drugs, such as cocaine. Every athlete at the games had to pee into a cup while a drug tester of the same sex watched. However, when I went to give my sample, I couldn't pee while the tester was watching. I left the small washroom and headed for the cooler in the stable, which always held an ample supply of bottled water. Returning to the bathroom half an hour later, I had no trouble producing a sample. Afterwards, I asked the drug tester why she had to be there, invading an expected and assumed privacy.

She told me that before the collection process was carefully monitored by having an attendant watch, it had been easy to substitute urine. The athletes just had to take other urine into the bathroom with them. She explained that this way was not foolproof either. At the last Olympics, a male athlete had somehow inserted a female's urine into his bladder. But he was caught—the urine he'd used was from a pregnant female!

The day before the opening ceremonies, the horses were shipped to Conyers, Georgia, where all the equestrian competitions were held. Grooms were housed in trailers on the site so that they were near the horses. Bussing was available to take the athletes to the equestrian site from the athletes' village at Georgia State University. At the village, the equestrian team members were allocated an old residence. The female shower facility was the men's locker room, consisting of one big room with multiple shower heads, so there was no privacy. Privacy was also hard to come by in the dorm rooms; each one had two or three inhabitants. The dorms were supposedly air-conditioned, but the Atlanta summer was stiflingly hot.

Security was tight at both the athlete's village and at the equestrian venue. Before the games started, we all had our right thumbprints scanned. Each time I came to the security gate at the entrance to the village or the equestrian venue, a scan was taken of my right thumb; it had to match the original one before I could enter the complex.

The dining facilities in the athletes' village were amazing. In an air-conditioned tent the size of a football field, you could choose from innumerable varieties of food, originating in every country imaginable. As well, you would have been more than happy with the array of choices available to you if you were a vegetarian or vegan, had religious food limitations, or if you had any type of voluntary or involuntary food restriction or allergy. A plethora of desserts was offered, along with every type of coffee.

As a member of the Canadian Olympic Team, I had been given pins to trade. Each country's pin design was unique and creatively designed. They were lapel pins, not campaign buttons, with intricate detail and brilliant color. The Canadian pins were tiny Canadian flags. I tried to get pins from smaller countries with fewer athletes. Since these were scarce, they were considered more valuable. I felt special because my birthday falls on the same day—April 10—that several pins were created to recognize the 100 days before the opening ceremonies. The pin-trading added a unique social element to my experience at the games and facilitated interaction with athletes from other countries who were taking part in other sports.

My favourite memory of the whole Olympic adventure is walking down the ramp into the Centennial Olympic Stadium during the opening ceremonies. Before parading in, all the athletes from every country participating sat waiting in the blistering heat in an old stadium right next door to the new one that was built for the Olympics. Munching on sandwiches, thankful for the water also provided by the organizers, we enjoyed watching the buildup to the athletes' parade on huge TV monitors that had been mounted in the stadium.

Athletes were called, country by country, to march into the Olympic stadium. The overflowing crowd, holding coveted tickets, was still very excited when it was our turn to enter the main stadium because C falls early in the alphabet. We followed the Canadian flag bearer, Charmaine Brookes, a runner who was a silver medallist at the 1984 Olympics in Los Angeles, into the stadium. As the Canadian athletes glided down the ramp, our tremendous pride was evident to all who were watching. Bolstered by the cheering crowd, we marched joyfully around the stadium track, waving enthusiastically the whole time.

Once we'd walked around the track, we joined the alphabetically preceding countries in the infield of the enormous stadium. Then, from our infield position, we watched D to Z enter the stadium, the athletes all wearing their countries' official Olympic uniforms. The crowd in the stadium burst into applause as each team flowed down the ramp where, moments before, we too had been parading into the limelight.

Underlining the enormity of the moment, some tiny countries were so sparsely represented that a sole athlete, who was also the flag bearer, marched into the stadium, waving enthusiastically to the cheering crowd. When the athletes had all entered the stadium and made their ways around its perimeter, the teams milled around in the infield in an organized chaos while the rest of the opening ceremonies took place. It was a huge party; we literally bumped into athletes from all around the world.

However, at the same time as I was revelling in the electric atmosphere of the infield, I felt the enormous expectations that were always weighing down on my shoulders become even heavier. Along with the expectations I always felt—those of my supporters, particularly my parents, and along with all the people who had helped me during my climb to the top—were now added the hopes of all Canadians. Canadians are terribly proud of their athletes. I was someone who had always felt the burden of the tremendous expectations that I presumed were emanating from my supporters. These expectations became a huge load for me to carry when I represented my country at the Olympics. I felt the already-heavy burden crushing me.

The opening ceremonies over, we hurried to catch one of the waiting buses back to the athlete's village. The horse inspection, always held the day before the first day of dressage, would start our competition the next day. From the athlete's village in downtown Atlanta, we'd have to catch a shuttle bus for the almost two-hour commute out to the equestrian venue at a very early hour the next morning.

At the equestrian facility, it was hot, hot, hot. Misters had been set up near the stabling area, each emitting a series of fine, gentle sprays, so you could stand a horse under them to cool off. The stabling tents were cooled off as much as possible with the use of fans and cooling mist. However, given their large body mass, horses are not efficient at dissipating heat. Long after the Olympics, Kim gave me a wonderful photograph of her standing under a mister holding Gordon and affectionately looking up at him. Both seemed to be enjoying the brief reprieve from the relentless heat. It made a great picture, but it did not represent the hard work and drive that had gotten Gordon, Kim and me to the games. Instead, it revealed the oppressive climate faced daily by all involved.

I got a terrible cold, possibly from being in enclosed spaces with many others or maybe from moving from the intense heat of Georgia in the summer into the too-cold air conditioning of the living and dining facilities at the equestrian park and in Atlanta. I saw the official physicians because I was all stuffed up, and they gave me some medicine. It was crucial to not take a prohibited drug, as many of the pills that one would normally take in such a situation were prohibited. The medicine I was given, keeping those rules in mind, did not relieve the symptoms at all.

I'm sure that for most athletes the village, which was situated in downtown Atlanta, was central. However, the equestrian competition was held very far away. The location meant that the riders faced a long ride in a bus every morning to get to the equestrian site at Conyers. Unless a house had been rented close by, the only option available was to bus back and forth. Renting a house was expensive, and I am sure that most teams' coffers were not deep enough to do so.

I will never forget the night I was awakened in the athletes' village in Atlanta, where I'd decided to stay for a couple of days after I'd finished competing. At around midnight I was jarred awake from my sound sleep, blinded by the light of a flashlight that our team leader was shining into the dark dorm room. She was making sure that we were all accounted for. A shooting had caused havoc during some Olympic activities downtown. I felt frightened and appalled that someone could threaten what we all held so dear and of which we were all so proud.

I didn't do well at the Olympics. Gordon and I received an average dressage score. The day after dressage, the competitors were faced with a cross-country course that was twisty and had slippery footing. I'd been on the course for less than a minute when Gordon slipped, falling right over on his side. Although the official who had seen the fall decided that I was not to be penalized, I was unaware of his decision, so I thought the fall would be counted. Much later in the course, I fell legitimately. Two falls means elimination. I understood from the official at the fence where I'd fallen the second time that I'd been eliminated, so I retired. Because I didn't complete the cross-country, I was not allowed to jump the following day.

For a team's score to count, at least three of its four members must complete the competition. Since another Canadian team member was also eliminated, only two of the four Canadians finished. We were no longer eligible for the team competition. I felt betrayed by what should have been the experience of a lifetime. Factors beyond my control—and believe me, I controlled everything I could—created insurmountable odds. Living arrangements, tremendous distances that had to be tackled daily, oppressive heat and far less-than-ideal galloping conditions on the cross-country course led to a very disappointing result.

The Canadian Olympic Committee Values "were established to remind athletes … that the life skills and experience obtained through athletic preparation, competition and teamwork are far more valuable than any medal ever awarded."[6] I certainly didn't feel that I had acquired the life skills of athletic preparation, competition and teamwork from competing at the Olympics. I'd added much more to my experience at other competitions. I'd gone to the Olympics with those skills already in place. I'd gone to do well, and I'd failed. I was inconsolably miserable.

The ultimate test, everything I had worked toward, had ended, and it had left a bitter taste in my mouth. Miserable, despondent and disheartened, I felt that I had not only let myself down but also Gordon and Kim, as well as my parents, my supporters and my country. Rereading the Olympic mission—"We believe that the short and long-term physical, social, mental and spiritual well-being of all should be enhanced through appropriate behavior and practices"[7]—didn't help at all. Instead, my Olympic experience had formed a crater in my mental well-being. It was years before I reconciled—somewhat—with the negative feelings that my Olympic experiences left behind.

All competitors were given passes to some other events. So I stayed in Atlanta for a couple of days to watch some heats of the swimming events. Then, picking up Gordon and Kim, I headed north to Canada to hang my head, stopping for the night in Virginia as I made my way home.

It's somewhat surprising to me, but I'm discovering and remembering a lot as I commit my memories to paper. However, I find that as I recount my memories of my mostly precious past, there are some of them, like my Olympic experiences, that I would rather forget. I keep them buried in my mind, but these unwanted memories tend to quietly fester just below the surface. Although they can't hurt me there, I do have to stomp on them occasionally, because although it happens infrequently, that painful time tends to try to re-irritate me. Now that I've acknowledged those scratchy memories by writing about them, I intend to bury them again—for good this time.

Now

For a long time, I've wondered why I spent so many years focused only on my equestrian life. Almost two decades later, it's become clear to me why I did this for so long: I hadn't yet accomplished what had been (albeit unconsciously) my goal since I was a child. I wanted to be successful as a member of the Canadian Equestrian Team. I'd done very well in North America, competing with my main men, Master Sing and Gordon Gibbons. But I hadn't done well—at all—at international competitions. I had never been good enough. Every time I'd competed internationally, I'd quietly shattered. My dreams remained just dreams. Sobbing silently inside, I would always try again.

Only in recent years have I at long last confronted what I've known for a long time: it wasn't only me who suffered the painful losses and disappointments during my years on the Canadian Equestrian Team. I've had to work through the feelings I had over letting down my parents too. I don't think that I'll ever completely reconcile my feelings of responsibility for their (imagined by me?) losses and disappointments. I do hope, however, that I'll keep coming closer.

Both Mom and Cruddums were so incredibly supportive throughout all those years, my mother accompanying me everywhere I went with the horses; she remained an integral part of my support team even when I was old enough to cope on my own. My father, perplexed as he was by my equestrian ambitions, was nonetheless always there for me, living my dreams in his own way. I'll always admire them for not asking the question that I was determined not to face: What was I planning to do next?

Coping

The sand is always damp in the early hours. Although the morning sun is still at half mast, it bounces off the dew coating my world. Gordon's hooves disturb the wet grass; the footsteps of our journey now revealed for all to see.

Although I felt devastated after the Atlanta Olympics, I was such a creature of habit that my January routine stayed the same. I went south to Southern Pines with five horses: Gordon, Sing, Hubcap, Freddie and Martin. For several years, I'd lived a nomadic lifestyle, dragging my belongings behind me in a spacious five-horse trailer. During that time, I'd always managed to dodge the real questions that I needed to consider: How long was I going to live this way, focused so narrowly on one goal? When was I going to settle down?

Equestrian sports, three-day eventing in particular, require so much dedication, so many lonely hours. It's hard for anyone who has not fallen under the sport's spell to understand how just a few shining moments can make everything seem worthwhile. Such moments are distributed sparsely. More frequently, riders endure disappointing periods that can go on for weeks. There are countless occasions when all their hard work seems to fly out the window.

Where had the years gone? I'd soon be 34 years old. It was high time I started to think about settling down, facing reality, being an adult. I knew that 1997 was a make-it-or-break-it year; it was time to produce a good result at an international competition. So I did all of the trials with the goal of being picked for "the team." *One last time*, I told myself. *Now or never.*

When I arrived in Southern Pines, the first thing I had to do was address my relationship with Harry. We had been coasting along for years, both of us self-centred, both of us doing our own thing, neither of us thinking more than a week ahead. We were living so in the moment. The future I saw ahead of us was not one I wanted to live for the long term.

I was dreading seeing Harry, but it turned out to be easy. When I pulled into the driveway of the farm where my barn was located, Harry was sitting on his horse talking to someone in the main barn. As I was parking, I saw him riding down the driveway on his horse, away from me. No hello. No "happy you're here." He must have been angry with me, but I had no clue why. That move, whether consciously or subconsciously performed on his part, ended our very unconventional relationship. When we talked later, we agreed to go our separate ways.

During January, I had a lesson with Gordon at eight thirty or nine each morning, mornings that were frequently bitterly damp and cold. It was often raining. Mike, Kim and I would see a car full of riders pass by on the road as I rode in Mike's ring under his careful scrutiny. We knew that the car's occupants were heading into town for breakfast. Mike was into birds; he watched them and knew about many kinds of birds. He called the carloads of riders "camper birds," saying that, like many birds, they had come south in the winter for the better weather. Camper birds were not used to doing any work in weather that was not sunny and warm. Since it was cold, they thought they might as well go for breakfast. It looked to us as if the camper birds viewed the whole Southern training experience as a lark. However, I had always ridden all day long in any type of weather. To everyone at my southern base, I must have seemed obsessed, but I don't think that they knew why. I'm sure that the other riders based in the area for the winter didn't understand me at all.

I'd lost a lot of weight during those winter months. I was skinny and very fit; there was not an ounce of fat on my body. It was a crazy time. I often felt as if I were crawling out of a dark place, scrambling, searching for footholds. In my worst moments, I was sure that any support holding me up would crumble away and leave me hanging, searching for a way out. It was the first time that I'd encountered such gloomy feelings. I don't think that I was clinically depressed, but I was floundering, envious of those around me—the camper birds!—who seemed to enjoy a much more level existence.

I'm not sure what kept me going during those dark days when I felt discouraged and had almost had enough. Although I never threw in the towel, miserable days stretched into dismal weeks. During those depressing periods, I dug deep within myself to search for the element that must be missing. I spent many days consumed by frustration as I tried to solve my problems, at the same time shouldering the heavy burden of all my supporters' hopes. Although I felt defeated and crushed after the Olympics, I always soldiered on, telling myself constantly to "suck it up, buttercup."

I struggled, I think with some success, to maintain a sunny exterior. I believe my emotions seemed fine to the outside world. Inside me, however, my mind churned in turmoil. Things such as an injured horse, or a horse that I couldn't coax to perform as well as he was able when it counted, were matters of colossal importance. In retrospect, I've no doubt that my perceptions were biased by my addled state of mind. At the time, it bothered me tremendously that, as far as I could tell, the other riders who were wintering in the area didn't seem to feel the pressures that I felt.

My parents were wonderful; I felt their support was there for me, although I refused to believe that they knew about these gloomy times. But they were parents, so no doubt they knew of my darkness and wondered what was going on. For years, my father has headed south for the month of March because the Canadian winter just goes on too long for him. At the end of that March, on his way home, he stopped by Southern Pines. It was unusual for him to do so; he always drove without stopping, was always in a hurry to get to where he was going. At the time I just thought it was great to see him; I now realize that I must have seemed different, distant, and so he felt it necessary to check on his daughter. But I was blinkered to the world outside my horses, so it didn't occur to me to wonder why he'd come by.

Something else happened during those crazy days. Most mornings, Mike would ride over and chat while I was grazing Hubcap. For just a short time, planning the day was put on hold, and we had time for each other. I enjoyed those chats, as I'm sure he did; it was a chance for a peaceful talk before we were captured by the day's busyness. When Hubcap's time was up, Mike rode back to his stable next door. Mike and I spent most of the day riding around each other. Because I often rode my horses over at his farm, our paths crossed many times during the day.

Mike and I grew closer, our conversations always entangled with our horses and the next competitions on the calendar. In the evenings, we would watch the day's videos that Kim had taken. Soon the conversations were continuing over dinner. I think that it was probably inevitable in my blinkered existence that we began to spend the night together. Although he was much older than I was, the relationship was respectful, comfortable and seemed so right at the time.

Gordon and me at the veterinary inspection. Rolex
Kentucky Three-Day Event, 1997.
Credit: Siegel Photography

Despite my precarious psychological state, my results in the spring competitions were spectacular. I won two out of the four competitions leading up to the Spring USA Championships held in April in Lexington, Kentucky. Finishing second there, I was the highest-placed foreign competitor, so Gordon and I were chosen by the Canadians to be on the team representing Canada at the 1997 Open European Three-Day Event Championships that would be held at Burghley, England. As far as I was concerned, my obsessive spring seemed to have paid off.

The awards ceremony. Rolex Kentucky Three-
Day Event, 1997. We placed 2nd.
Credit: Siegel Photography

After competing at Kentucky, I went home to Canada. During the summer, I occasionally took the horses to Hamilton, Massachusetts so that I could train with Mike at his summer location. He flew to Canada once or twice to see me and to check on how Gordon and I were doing.

I was completely focused on my riding, so much so that I was initially completely unaware that my parents were less than thrilled about my relationship with Mike. Looking back, I think that they still hoped that the horsey part of my life would evolve and become only one part of who I was, that I would eventually acknowledge a few of the multitude of things, besides horses, that life had to offer. But I thought that being with Mike was wonderful; the relationship suited who I was at that point in my life. I was completely immersed in my horses and everything about them.

Secondly, Mike was much older than I was; his three sons were not that much younger than I was. I was 34 when we got together, he 57. I saw no problem with that. I was oblivious to anything in the world but my horses. It didn't occur to me that it was an unusual relationship.

In late August, the Canadian team spent about two weeks training at a farm in Toronto that had great stabling, dressage rings, fields to condition in and lots of jumps. At long last we had the opportunity to spend time together as a team. The riders and grooms were billeted at bed and breakfasts in the area. I found it interesting that, as usually happened in team situations, we all operated as individuals, with our own grooms and on our own schedules. There was little team camaraderie. Although I don't remember much of the precompetition training camp, what does stand out for me is August 31, the night before we left Canada to go to the competition in England. Rooms had been reserved for us at a hotel close to the Toronto airport. Although it's a useless bit of information, I'll always know exactly when the team flew to England. It was the day Princess Diana died.

The hotel gym had no treadmill, so I couldn't run. I was disappointed, because running was one of the most effective tools I had in my arsenal. I used it several times a week when I wasn't travelling, to expend energy that I otherwise would have spent worrying. I jumped on a StairMaster instead, but I soon stopped because I hate the things. Climbing those steps has always seemed like a contrived form of exercise to me.

Back in the room, I treated myself to room service. When dinner arrived, I nestled comfortably into bed, wearing a T-shirt and sweatpants, a tray of food balanced over my lap. Intent on finding a cheerful movie on TV that didn't require me to think, I didn't make it past the first channel, the one to which the TV was already tuned. There, I watched the horrifying story of Princess Diana's accident unfold. The story had taken over the TV. Although I subsequently flipped endlessly through the plethora of stations, the same story just repeated itself as the evening deepened and became early morning. When I finally switched off the TV, it was long after midnight. After only sleeping for a few hours, I didn't wait for the alarm before I turned on the TV, and I heard the unimaginably ghastly news—Diana had died.

The next morning the horses, their riders, their grooms and masses of equipment flew across the Atlantic and landed at Heathrow in London, England. We were picked up by a group of people from the horse trials at Burghley who had a van for the horses and cars for us. Mike arrived a week later, a few days before the competition was to begin. I was happy to see him; his presence made it more possible for Gordon and me to fall into a routine that felt comfortable and familiar.

But Mike and I were both very aware that it was anybody's guess how this team competition would unfold.

SEPTEMBER 13, 1997

Burghley, England

The cross-country course, which Mike and I had walked several times over the past couple of days, seemed more difficult than I expected it to be. There were many combinations; tricky questions faced the competitors very early on. Gordon passed the initial vet inspection. We did an average dressage test; next, speed and endurance loomed. At that time, phases A, B and C came before the cross-country. A and C were Roads and Tracks, with the pace averaged to a trot speed. B was the Steeplechase, which was done at a fast gallop over eight of the types of fences one would find at a race meet.

When competitors had completed phases A, B and C, but before setting out on phase D, the cross-country, there was a ten-minute rest period. During that time,

Jumping one of the steeplechase fences at the 1997 European Championships.
Credit: Renée Smith

horses were washed with water to cool them down, equipment was adjusted, and the horses were checked by a veterinarian.

Two minutes before I'm to go cross-country, I vault onto Gordon, who's always semicrazed right before his start on cross-country. Kim can barely keep up as we bounce toward the start box, but she's just able to hold onto a long leather shank that's attached to the halter she has slipped over his bridle. Like a bird, Gordon is ready to fly. I'm focused only on the job ahead of me. Nervous anticipation courses through my body.

Let's go. I'm ready.

It's impossible to sit calmly on this animal who feels as if he's about to explode. Holding both reins in my right hand, I tuck my riding whip between the saddle and my left thigh. My left hand now free, I reach up to tuck an imaginary wayward strand of hair under my helmet and unnecessarily adjust the plastic piece of the chinstrap that snugly cups my lower jaw. Finished fidgeting, I slide the whip out from under my leg so it rests along Gordon's shoulder and reposition my hand on the dripping, rubber-covered reins. Gordon is soaked in nervous sweat. A horse with his experience knows that phase D, the cross-country, is next.

I take a deep breath. I think of nothing but the challenge I'm about to face. Filling my lungs till I can't fit in any more air—till my safety vest strains against my chest—I visualize the challenging fourth fence.

Compress to a short, bouncy canter.

Jump.

Eyes, eyes, eyes to very narrow next element.

I slowly breathe out. All the air has to leave. Empty those lungs. I do the same exercise again.

Come on, it's time to get going.

Trying to comfort Gordon, I scratch his withers with my fingers while still holding onto the reins, but I know that it's all for naught. I'm sitting on top of a bubbling volcano.

The starter calls my number: "One-oh-seven, you have one minute."

"One-oh-seven, 30 seconds."

When he calls out 10 seconds, Kim leads us into the small, three-sided start box, its open end facing the course ahead. She circles Gordon, who by now is dancing, threatening to unseat me any moment. He knows what's going to happen next and can hardly wait to gallop away. The starter counts down the last five seconds.

"Five." I start my stopwatch.

"Four."

"Three."

"Two." Kim turns Gordon to the front of the box.

"One." She lets him go.

"Go"!

As if shot from a cannon, Gordon erupts out of the box. When the loudspeakers crackle into action, I can barely hear the announcer's voice: "Number 107, Claire Smith and Gordon Gibbons, have just left the start box."

Once on course, Gordon is, as always, all business. He immediately relaxes, settling into a rhythmic gallop as he moves quickly and economically across the ground. The noise produced by his pounding hooves is somewhat softened by the long-established grass that blankets the parkland of this estate in Burghley, England.

Gordon's pricked ears frame the path I've planned precisely on my many walks around the daunting track that awaits us. I've jumped each fence over and over in my mind, visualizing how I'm going to ride different parts of the cross-country course.

Shortly after bursting out of the start box, we approach the first fence, a stack of wooden barrels. Gordon flies effortlessly over it and then over the second, a little log house that even has a stone chimney climbing the wall and a flower bed running along its front. Cheering crowds line the galloping lanes, here to watch the best riders in the world attempt to ride cleanly and quickly around one of the most challenging courses of the year, but I don't hear them. I'm completely focused on the job at hand. Years of high-level competition have enabled me to shut out these distractions.

The third obstacle is another straightforward effort, made up of huge timbers. Just outside the white flag marking the left-hand side of the area through which the horses must jump, a large realistic-looking, but wooden, circular saw decorates the fence, poised to carve the massive timbers into planks. The jump is soon behind us.

Less than a minute after our start, Gordon and I gallop toward the combination at fence four, the first serious question asked by the course designer. Many spectators are gathered here; this is one of the most difficult obstacles on the course. Squeezed tightly against the course ropes that have been put there to keep them away from the jumps, they're anxiously waiting to watch me negotiate this tricky combination. Although I know they're there, I'm completely zoned in on the difficult task I'm about to face.

Slowing down, I compress Gordon's gallop until his stride is short and bouncy. We reach the first element: a sloping jump made of three enormous logs. It's poised on the edge of a steep bank, so from the takeoff side it looks as if we're about to leap into the sky. Leaning back as Gordon jumps, I let the reins slip through my fingers, allowing his neck to stretch forward. He scrambles more than 30 feet down until he reaches the bottom of the bank.

I know Gordon very well, so when we get to the level ground, I'm concerned because he feels unsure. Unlike their riders, horses see the course for the first time when they are competing over it. They must completely rely on their riders to guide them around, showing them where to go and what pace they need for the current challenge. Gordon has always been confident on a cross-country course, so I can usually count on him to quickly size up almost every question asked of him. He zeroes in on what he must do as soon as he sees the fence in front of him. But this time Gordon feels unfocused; I don't think he understands the jump, the question being asked. I'm very tuned into everything his body tells me, so when he hesitates for a split second, I sense that he's confused.

We have only a couple of strides on the flat before we have to jump the narrow fence ahead of us. I don't have enough time at this late stage to change my plan and instead go the longer, more time-consuming but easier, way to complete the obstacle. Two short strides don't leave my already-rattled horse enough time to understand what is being asked of him.

Unable to figure it out, Gordon desperately launches himself into the air. When he leaves the ground, his jumping form, usually classic and safe, is anything but. His knees dangle toward the ground so he catches his front legs, and he somersaults over the jump.

Down we go.

CHAOS

Chaos is the ultimate muteness that forces speech to go faster and faster, trying to catch the suffering in words.[8]

Horror

September 13, 1997
Burghley, England
Claire's Mother, Renée

My husband, Brad, and I are both at the competition to watch our daughter ride. Brad flew over at the last minute; I can't begin to tell you how thankful I am that he's here. Although very proud of his daughter's equestrian accomplishments, he attends very few of the competitions. It's always taken a bit of persuasion, but so far I've managed to get him to come to the big ones: the 1994 World Championships in Holland and the 1996 Olympics in Atlanta.

I'm with Claire's coach and best friend, Mike, in the competitors' tent, anxiously anticipating watching her ride the whole course on the five closed-circuit TVs crowded into the tent. At major competitions, a tent is located near the start and finish of cross-country. It's restricted to competitors, their grooms, their coaches and the owners of the horses competing. Riders yet to start, as well as support teams, can keep a close eye on several television monitors displaying live footage of the riders on course. Sometimes competitors with later start times see that the way they are planning to negotiate an obstacle is not working well for others already on course. They can then make last-minute changes to their plans for that obstacle.

"Here, let's sit here." Mike slides onto the nearest collapsible metal chair. The chairs, resting unevenly on the grass floor of the tent, face the TVs, each one crackling with a grainy black-and-white live image of a rider from a different point on the course. Members of the anxious audience are restlessly seated, in turn clapping, gasping or groaning expressively. There's applause for each rider crossing through the finish flags.

By the time Mike and I sit down, Claire and Gordon are already halfway down the bank at obstacle four. We perch precariously on the edges of our tippy chairs, our eyes glued to the monitor following the pair. At the bottom of the bank, Gordon hesitates. We watch in horror as he flips over the next jump.

Gordon hits the ground hard, landing upside down on the other side of the jump. Grunting loudly as the air is suddenly smacked out of his lungs, he lies quietly on his back for a couple of seconds while he regains his breath. Then he quickly and frantically scrambles until he's upright, his feet churning up the centuries-old turf on which the course is built. While he's getting back onto his feet, Gordon carefully avoids touching Claire where she's lying beside him. We'll forever be thankful that when he fell over the fence, Gordon ended up next to her, not on top of her. The story would have ended tragically had that been the case.

"Oh my God!" When he sees Claire fall, Mike jumps up, knocking over his chair and dashing from the competitors' tent toward the fourth fence. An experienced eight-time Olympian representing the United States, he's all too aware that the fall looks very serious. He's terrified when he sees Claire, who is not only his student but also his partner, lying motionless on the grass. Following him more slowly, I'm not fully aware of the gravity of the situation.

At large competitions, there is usually a helicopter poised to fly to the scene in case of an accident on course. When the paramedics realize it's needed, they fly it to the fourth fence, landing it in a space cleared of spectators by the officials.

When I reach the jump and see the ambulance crew huddled around Claire's prone figure, all my motherly instincts rush to the fore.

"Let me through! I'm her mother! If you don't, I'll scream." I can't believe it; this is a nightmare. I've seen some serious falls, but this time it's my daughter. The ambulance crew warn me not to touch her as I fall to my knees on the muddied, trampled grass on the landing side of the narrow jump. I'm as close as I can get to her; they can't stop me from desperately whispering in her ear, "I'm here. Dad's here. We love you!"

She just lies there. Face down. Immobile.

Amazingly, a neurologist happens to be standing by the next obstacle. He makes his way quickly to Claire's side when he hears over the loudspeaker that there has been a fall at the previous jump and that there is now a hold on the course, meaning that subsequent competitors are stopped. Under the neurologist's careful watch, the ambulance crew immediately intubate Claire, enabling them to give her drugs to artificially paralyze her. Then the crew are forced to wait for the drugs to take effect; they don't want her to move in case she's broken her neck. It seems to take forever, but finally they place Claire on a stretcher and load her into the waiting helicopter.

Unconscious and unaware of everything, our daughter flies peacefully over England in an air ambulance. Below her lies the snarled highway along which Mike, Brad and I are chauffeured toward the hospital in an official vehicle from the competition. Because of roadwork, our progress is excruciatingly slow. I'm so frantic that I'm about to jump out and run. The car only inches forward, starting and stopping the whole way. Endless scenarios relentlessly play in my head.

Quick!

Hurry!

Faster!

Knowing Brad, it doesn't surprise me that, despite the horrendous occasion, he remains practical as the terrible day continues to unfold. He phones his cousin, a radiologist in London.

"Shirley, it's Brad. Claire's had a horrific fall. We're on the way to the hospital." Shirley assures him that the hospital in Nottingham and its doctors are excellent.

The air ambulance arrives at the hospital a couple of hours before we do, the pilot carefully lowering the helicopter and touching it down softly onto the landing pad. Then the waiting emergency crew, accustomed to incoming air ambulances, quickly unload Claire. They whisk her away to undergo a thorough examination by a team of doctors who have been alerted to her impending arrival. The doctors carefully X-ray her back and neck from every possible angle so that they can figure out what parts of her are broken.

Claire's body, silenced by the drugs the paramedics had given her at the competition, is completely still and remains that way for the next couple of days as doctors continue to administer the same drugs. No one is sure whether she has severed her spinal cord; until they determine what is amiss, it's crucial that she be kept immobile and sedated.

By the time we finally make it to the hospital after the seemingly endless journey, I'm beside myself. Leaping out of the car before it stops rolling, we all forget to thank the driver before we rush into the emergency department. Leaning over the reception desk just inside the door, I frantically ask the nurse sitting there how Claire is, sobbing and demanding to see her. "I'm her mother. Tell me how she is—let me see her!"

However, the nurse has no news on Claire's condition, so she leads us to the hospital waiting room, where tired chairs covered with thin vinyl padding line the walls. The outdated magazines scattered on a table in the corner of the room are well thumbed, their covers wrinkled and torn. Neither the hard chairs nor the old magazines offer us any comfort. Impatiently, we wait for news from the doctors. Why doesn't someone come to update us? Unable to sit, we pace the room in disbelief.

A mother in crisis, my emotions are in overdrive. *Is this a nightmare? Will someone please wake me up!*

Brad stares blindly into the vending machine. "Do you want a coffee?"

It is the last thing I need or want. *How about a stiff drink instead?*

Several hours into the night—a seemingly interminable time after the fall—Brad and I finally see our daughter for the first time. Claire is immobile, lying perfectly still in a hospital bed, her face bloodied. Both her eyes are closed, and it's obvious that her right eye wouldn't open even if she wanted it to; it's black and blue, swollen shut. She's a horrifying sight, but at least we witness first-hand that she's still breathing, so we know that she's alive.

It's incredibly comforting to know that she is still with us, but I can't begin to describe how awful the next couple of days are. They run together into an endless living chaos. We subsist in a daze of disbelief and worry.

What's happening?

This isn't real … it's not, is it?

Oh God …

Claire's right collarbone, broken when she fell, seems trivial in the grand scheme of things. What about her neck, her back? We are barely hanging in there, bracing ourselves for awful news. What if she has broken her neck and will be in a wheelchair for the rest of her life? Everyone at the hospital is very kind.

"We've got a bed in the room adjacent to Claire's if you'd like to stay," a nurse kindly asks. It's nice to hear that because there's no way I'll leave the hospital. Neither will Brad. Or Mike, for that matter.

Unable to sleep, we spend the night sitting vigilantly at Claire's bedside. Exhaustion and horrendous imaginings etch our faces. Days and nights run together; time no longer governs anyone's world.

September 15, 1997
Nottingham, England
Renée

It seems that years have gone by since that horrible day, but it's only about two days later. Claire's condition seems not to have changed. Brad and I are sitting in our daughter's hospital room when I'm sure that I see the sheet covering Claire's legs move. "Did you see that?"

Brad's eyes lift from his book when he hears my excited voice, and then we both see her move her legs again!

"Thank God, thank God!" Breaking down in tears, we're both desperate to ask her to move her legs once more so that we can be sure of what we've seen, but this momentous event occurs when Claire's still barely conscious and not communicating. The intubated drugs are only partially out of her system. Seeing for myself that she's not paralyzed, I can finally thank God and stop imagining the worst. I'm no longer haunted by the image of the interior of Claire's house, which I've redesigned endlessly in my mind to be wheelchair accessible for her.

After determining that Claire's neck isn't broken, the doctors focus on their accompanying diagnosis: a severe traumatic brain injury (TBI). I've heard lots of comments over the years: "I must have hit my head; I can't believe what I just did …" This flippant remark, or one very similar, is usually made by people to excuse themselves after a faux pas. It reveals how little knowledge most people (which at this point includes Brad and me) have about head injury and its consequences. Ignorant as we are, Brad and I have no idea what we're about to face.

We're not left in the dark for too long. When Claire's doctors tell us what their initial assessments reveal, the awfulness of the situation becomes almost intolerable. Her fall has—probably—left her with significant cognitive, physical, emotional and physiological damage. There's little doubt in their minds that the head injury will cause behavioral changes. Terrified, Brad and I listen to what they have to say. Then we can only hopelessly imagine what lies ahead of us.

Horrifying images of what we—Brad and I and Claire—will go through soon take over my mind. My expectations of what is to follow get quickly worse when, after listening to the doctors' doom-and-gloom predictions, I read as much as I can get my hands on.

> Physical functions can be affected, such as standing, walking and eye-hand coordination. Cognitive changes can include issues with memory and language. Personality traits can be affected. People may lose their

natural inhibitions and behavior control, leading to inappropriate behavior. The effects of a brain injury can be extremely widespread, impacting all areas of a person's life and requiring extensive medical and rehabilitative treatment.[9]

Will my daughter now only slightly resemble the girl I've raised, the bright, confident individual I know so well? I'm not sure that I can bear it.

September 1997
Nottingham, England
Renée

The hotel where I stay for the first few days of this hell is quite a distance through town. Then I find a bed and breakfast that's only a 10-minute walk from the hospital, so I no longer need to rent a car. The immediate problem I face is that, when I left home, I'd packed only a week's worth of clothes. Although I'm usually an enthusiastic shopper, when I walk to the nearest department store I find that I have a complete lack of interest. In every way, my world has turned colourless and depressed, my thoughts narrowly focused only on my daughter.

I faithfully make my way up the street every morning to spend the day at the hospital with Claire, the journey growing even greyer and bleaker as October draws near. Each day the wind is increasingly bitter and blustery, sombrely warning of even colder weather soon to come. Unfailingly, it wraps its chilly arms around me as I make the short trek to the hospital. These walks are adding to my depression. It's late fall, so the trees lining the street are slowly undressing. They're soon bare, their dead leaves fluttering to the ground and lying either crispy underfoot on the sidewalk or lounging like sodden rags in the gutters.

When I get to the hospital, I take a deep breath and slowly climb up the wide concrete steps at the main entrance of the old brick building. The approach to the heavy wooden doors of the hospital has become part of my daily routine. Just inside the door, the nurse sitting behind the sliding glass window at the information booth knows me by now.

"Good morning, Mrs. Smith. It's crisp out, but at least it's not raining."

Making my way across the bustling hospital lobby, I stride by a cluster of people standing around waiting for the "lift." No elevators here; it's England. I hear the lift descending, making its way down to the main floor as I pull open the stairwell door situated to its left. Although I always take the stairs, no one else seems to. It's almost guaranteed that I won't meet anyone on my way up. The lift's doors noisily clatter open, audible through the thin hospital walls of the stairwell. I climb past the second floor, where doctors have their offices. The third floor is the neonatal unit. Through the small window in the stairwell door, I see a young couple the lift has just discharged, anxiety etched across their faces. The lift rattles and whines on its way up to the respiratory unit on four, so I know I'm keeping pace with it. When I arrive at five, neurology, I realize how "lucky" we are that Claire is a floor up in the orthopedic unit because she broke her collarbone in the fall—even though the break is inconsequential in light of the head injury. Six is a lot quieter and infinitely more peaceful than the neurology unit on five, which is typically home to loud, disturbed voices.

When I reach the sixth floor, I pull open the door. I feel a tiny bit of pathetic satisfaction—I need it during this awful time—because I've beaten the lift; its doors are just opening. My shoulders drop as I exhale the breath that I don't even realize I've been holding for much of the journey up the stairs. Turning right, I walk slowly along the now familiar hall, its artificial brightness a stark contrast to the gloomy, overcast October weather outside. Claire's room is opposite the nurses' station, just a short distance from the stairs. Although post-traumatic amnesia silences any new memories Claire might make, she seems to know me and is always happy to see me. When I finally figure out how her memory is working, I realize that I am a *before*—before the accident on September 13, before Claire's time stood still, before each day began trickling seamlessly into the next.

September 1997
Burritts Rapids, Ontario
Claire's Father, Brad

The flight back from England is endless. It takes about seven and a half hours, daylight the whole way. I'm on the same plane as the Canadian Equestrian Team horses. Because they're cargo, horses fly in a transport plane. Some, as is this one, are "combis," half passengers, half cargo.

Although the plane left London Heathrow airport at 1 p.m., we're not only flying into the wind but also against the five-hour time change, so the clocks say it's only two and a half hours later when we finally land in Toronto. I'm lucky that I'm able to sleep a bit, despite the cramped airplane seats. The stewardess's voice jars me awake as we begin our descent: "Please ensure all electronic devices, including laptop computers and computer games, are turned off." I follow these standard directions; soon the plane jostles my seat gently as it touches down on the runway and she announces our arrival: "Welcome to Toronto. The local time is 3:33 p.m."

Claire's horse trailer is parked in a locked yard, which turns out to be miles away from the airport. Squished uncomfortably in a cheap, tiny rental car for the hour-long trek to retrieve the rig, I wonder why the trailers are parked so far away. My day has already been far too long, and I still have to go back to the airport to get Gordon. Then, it's a good four-hour drive home to our farm in Burritts Rapids, which lies 45 minutes southwest of Ottawa.

When I finally make it home, it's dark, and the answering machine is full:

"Hi, Brad and Renée, just thinking about you both. If you need anything at all, please don't hesitate to call."

"Renée, I won't bother you, but if you want any help at all, you know how to reach me."

"I guess you're not home yet. Unbelievable news. Shattering. What can I do?"

The next day the phone rings constantly. I am inundated with calls from all over, and I feel comforted by the huge outpouring and offers of help from Claire's friends, my friends and many acquaintances. People I don't even know call just to say that they're thinking of us. From all parts of Claire's life, as well as from Renée's and mine, people are offering every kind of help. Among these calls was one from a local stable owner who kindly suggested that I send not just Gordon but also the five horses Claire had left at home to board with them.

I'm an automaton. Thank goodness I can go to the office. But, after a couple of weeks, I can't stand it anymore, so I fly back to England. Poor Renée has been there alone; she needs my support. The six-and-a-half-hour flight leaves Montreal at night and gets to London first thing in the morning. Because it's with the wind, you skip a night and, unless you're able to close your eyes in the cramped economy class seat, its sleep. Bumping down through heavy cloud cover into Heathrow, it doesn't help my mood that it's overcast and drizzling. Jet-lagged and finding it hard to stay awake, I make my way through a depressing area around Leeds on the monotonous two-hour drive to Nottingham.

When I get to the hospital to see my daughter, I don't take the elevator. Instead, as does my wife during this unimaginably difficult time, I bounce up the stairs, although I realize that it's only a nod to my need for exercise. It's eight steps up to the landing, then I turn hard right and sprint up eight more steps to the next floor. Reaching the sixth floor, I make my way along the hall until I reach Claire's room. Striding purposefully in, I sit with Claire, freeing up her mother so that she can spend her day touring the less-than-exciting streets of Nottingham. I'm encouraged; although Claire is enveloped by post-traumatic amnesia, she's started to walk, albeit very unsteadily.

While I'm there, Claire has an appointment with the neurologist.

"Okay, are you ready?" I ask Claire who, of course, doesn't have a clue what to be ready for. I'm having trouble figuring out how her mind is working, but I do know that since she seems only to be in the present moment, she has no idea that she was told yesterday about the appointment. Because the wheelchair doesn't "do" stairs, we take the lift down to the second floor, where the doctors' offices are located. There, the waiting room prompts unwelcome flashbacks: my mind flies back to September 13 because this waiting room is just like the one we spent endless hours in on that horrible day.

"All set for lunch?" I ask Claire when her appointment's over. I realize that the question is pointless, but I keep hoping she'll return to us. We take the lift down to the main floor, where the cafeteria is located. Pushing the wheelchair with my left hand, I slide the tray along the counter with my right. The staff of the cafeteria hand me the soup of the day—mushroom. It startles me to see that they all wear white cotton gloves, reminiscent of the previous century.

I've always wondered about all that riding, all those horses. From day one, when she decided to pursue her goal full time, Claire's been so focused, so driven. She's so bright, she should have continued her education. I told her, though, a couple of years ago, that I didn't understand why she spent all her time with the horses, but if she was happy, I was happy too.

Damn horses.

October 1997
Nottingham, England
Renée

Claire's still in the hospital at Nottingham, and it's become October. I can't wait for her to be flown back to Canada; however the doctors want to make sure she is stable before sending her to a hospital near our home. Late one afternoon, I walk into her hospital room. My dripping raincoat is evidence of the dreary weather outside.

"How was your day?" my husband asks. "Oh, look at you; I guess it's raining again. Claire said something very clearly just now. I was amazed." Because I know him so well, I can tell he's a little excited. Brad has been with our daughter most of the day, ensconced in a chair he has strategically placed by the door to discourage her from wandering into the hall. She can hardly walk, but this fact does not seem to deter her, as her father has presumably discovered. Even though Claire's playpen-like bed has railings that are about three feet high, she can easily climb over them, making it essential that someone sit with her all the time.

"I was sitting here, trying not to nod off—do you find it very warm in here? Anyway, I guess I did fall asleep, because I opened my eyes to see Claire standing very unsteadily in the bathroom. She was looking in the mirror and, clear as day, she said, 'Black eye.' I find it fascinating! It's the only time she's made any sense to me."

Since the accident, Claire has been talking gibberish; we can't understand a word of her nonsensical ramblings. Even if she did make sense, she'd be hard to understand because her speech is very thick and slurred.

"Did she eat anything?" I ask Brad as he slowly unfolds himself out of the chair. "We've got to get her to eat more. She's far too thin."

"There must be a better chair that they can lend us. This thing hurts my back. No, but the doctor stopped in and didn't seem worried when I mentioned our concern to him."

For six interminable weeks, Claire's been a patient in the Nottingham hospital. Brad and her brothers, John Willem and Philip, make a couple of trips over to see her, but I suspect that these trips are primarily to keep an eye on me. After witnessing Claire's horrendous fall, although on a TV, I'm having to bear the day-to-day reality of the weeks immediately following her accident. My once competent, independent daughter needs help with everything. Claire no longer has the very rudimentary skills of life.

Claire can't talk or walk. Now that she's finally started using the toilet again, she announces at least once every hour that she needs to go. Together, we make the journey across the room; it takes all my strength to support her as she weaves unsteadily toward the bathroom. When we finally get there, I'm not at all surprised that, like a child being toilet-trained, she often just sits there and nothing happens. Even though she's 34 years old, she's become my child again. And I've become a bit like a mother bear and will do anything to protect my baby.

This hell is not what life, what living, is supposed to be all about. Why, oh why did this happen?

To get my daughter out so she sees more than her room's four walls, I spend hours pushing Claire's wheelchair through the hospital, exploring its every corner. My shoes clatter behind the chair's silently rolling wheels as I trudge along countless corridors made up of cold, sombre grey linoleum floors harshly lit by fluorescent lighting that seems to bounce too eagerly off the puce-green walls. The kind people at the bed and breakfast pack me a lunch every day, so Claire and I can eat together. But before I eat, I feed Claire. As I spoon the boring hospital food into her mouth, I'm thankful that she seems unaware of its bland taste and greyish-yellowish colouring, as well as its paste-like texture.

My days at the hospital are endlessly long. It's devastating to see my once competent, self-assured daughter reduced to a baby-like state. Radiating confidence, the treating neurologists tell me that her brain can compensate for the injury. In a year, they tell me, no one will notice that anything happened to her. The doctors insist that, although the brain was once thought to be a hard-wired and static entity, it's now known that it can rewire itself after injury. This is because of the neuroplasticity of the brain, which is "defined as the ability for neuronal circuits to make adaptive changes on both a structural and functional level, ranging from molecular, synaptic and cellular changes to more global network changes."[10]

Yeah, right … really? It's hard to believe, considering that everything I've found in the Nottingham library is full of doom and gloom about severe head injury. It's all shattering; it seems that Claire will not at all be like the Claire we knew. The reading I've done suggests that with early treatment—which all sources underscore is essential for traumatic and severe brain injuries—the future quality of Claire's life can be improved in several ways. However, the forecast for those who have sustained a severe head injury is so depressing; the percentages of individuals who successfully rehabilitate are only in the teens.

The articles and books all indicate that my daughter will be offered just a semblance of life as she lived it before her accident. The predictions for her return to independence—that is, her ability to live with minimal to moderate to no support in a home, group home or nursing-home setting—seem optimistic. But the details indicate that only a small percentage of survivors of severe head injury achieve total independence. The terms *group home* and *nursing home* fly out to meet me, leaving me despondent. It sounds as though her return to meaningful life activities, such as work, school or volunteer activities is highly unlikely. All I can focus on is what hasn't been said: she may not be able to pursue a career. In addition, the studies predict that her social life will be very changed. She may not be able to regulate her behavior, and so she may not be able to successfully maintain her independence.[11]

What's happened to my daughter? Surely I can expect more? Please ...

"Hi, Claire. Do you know what day it is?" I'm silently amazed when I hear the neurologist ask my daughter this question. I usually don't know what day it is when things are "normal." And now, life is so far from normal.

"I see you've been eating—that's great! And your mom has been pushing you around the hospital in a wheelchair, so you've been able to look around and see where you are." I roll my eyes. I know that although Claire seems to be looking at her surroundings, she has no idea that she's a patient in a hospital, no inkling where she is or how she got to where she is.

When the doctor asks, "Do you know why you're here?" I'm floored. Suddenly I realize that he isn't at all aware of what is glaringly clear to me: Claire obviously doesn't have a clue.

"Okay, you're doing wonderfully. See you in the morning." The neurologist strides out of the room, doesn't stop to ask me how it's going.

What about me! How am I doing? Well, since you're asking, I'll admit things are pretty dismal. My daughter is about six months old again.

During those hectic, painful days when no one is sure what will happen next, friends of mine living in England quickly come to be by my side and to lend moral support. Although good friends are nearby and Brad has flown to England a couple of times, all I can see is my severely injured daughter. My commitments back in Canada seem trivial. Brad can cope on his own for a while. Even if it had been June, when the garden always takes up all of my time, Claire's injury has wiped everything else from my mind.

It will be months—years?—before Claire realizes that her life has instantly and dramatically changed as a result of the fall. Thankfully, she is completely unaware of this awful truth: she doesn't understand the consequences of what has happened. We'll have to wait quite a while before we gently tell her that her life will have to be different. Of course, it would be better if she slowly discovered herself that horses can no longer be the centre of her life. There is no point in confronting her with her life's harsh realities while post-traumatic amnesia rules her world. Despite the doctors' sunny predictions, she has no idea who she is, why she's in the hospital or what has happened. She doesn't think about her future: she has no idea that there is a future. I don't quite understand how her mind is working, but I do know that she's always in the present moment.

As for me; I certainly didn't plan my way of being, but it seems as if I've emotionally shut down so that I'm more able to cope with the dreadful situation. By living without emotion, albeit an unconscious decision, I can guard against feeling anything, thereby readying myself for the next blow. Typical of the emotional vacuum I've become, I avoid anything that could reach out and provoke any sort of spontaneous and unrehearsed response. I'm only just surviving. My life is now just a haze of indistinguishable days that run together, each one nearly the same as the next.

Realizing that it's essential that I exercise—more than up the hospital stairs—I walk for at least an hour a day. Some days I head briskly into the nearby Nottingham University botanical gardens, needing to see colour, to witness birth and growth. However, because it's fall, the gardens are only a faded reminder of their summer glory. There's no inspiring growth and greenness to be seen.

"Oh, you're back! There's been a heavy mist and rain all day; it's very dark and gloomy out." The lady who runs the bed and breakfast welcomes me and then bends down to stoke the smoldering fire. She adds new logs and gently coaxes a healthy flame, bringing the sleeping fire back to life.

"Here, let me take that jacket. It needs to be draped over a chair right in front of the fire."

Shivering and rubbing my hands together, I pull off my sodden jacket, leaving puddles of water on the tiled kitchen floor as I do so.

"I'll hang the jacket, thanks. No need for you to get wet too." I linger in front of the fire, my toes tingling as they slowly thaw.

"I'm sure you'd like a cup of tea. So how is she? Better?"

I never know how to respond to that dreaded question. *Much better, thanks. She walked briskly down the hall, and we had an interesting intellectual conversation as we walked. We were out for over an hour.* No.

Instead, I tell Mrs. Bed-and-Breakfast that Claire's going to be all right, that the doctors have all told us that no one will notice anything after a year. That doesn't work either. I can't believe it, but hot tears push against my eyes. When I can't hold them in any longer, they spill out onto my cheeks.

"Oh, my dear. I'm sorry. Here. Move a chair right up to the stove and sit there for a while. You'll be in for dinner?"

I have nowhere to go. My world is my daughter. "Yes. Thanks. That would be so nice."

November 1997
The Ottawa Hospital
Brad

At the end of October, Claire is flown from England to a hospital near our home, in Ottawa, Canada. Renée and I are on the same flight, our seats in the row ahead of where she's sitting. We're very impressed; the doctor and a nurse sitting adjacent to Claire don't drug her in hopes of keeping her quiet. Instead, they quietly engage with her by talking and playing simple games. 'I spy' comes to mind. They reward her with incentives for good behavior, much as one would a young child. As a result, the flight is peaceful; at one point she even falls asleep. An ambulance meets the plane and takes her to the Ottawa Hospital. It will be her home until Christmas.

As I've done every day for the past month since Claire's been back in Canada, I detour by the hospital on my way home after a long day at the office and feed her two dinners. She's far too thin.

"Hello. Hello!" My kiss floats through the air close to her cheek. The frigid air that I've brought into the room with me curls around both of us. Although my arms are covered in snow, I'm not at all discouraged from wrapping them around my daughter. Some of the accumulated snow that's clinging to my jacket drifts to the floor next to her bed. Without thinking, I brush off more of the snow before I hang my jacket on the back of the room's door. Piled up on the floor right next to Claire's bed, the snow will soon melt into slippery puddles.

"Oh, bother. It's just starting to snow. Did your mother take you on an outing today?" I ask her, even though I know she doesn't remember that her mother pushed her in a wheelchair outdoors around the hospital grounds a few hours ago. Renée takes her outside every morning.

"Here, I'll crank the bed up a bit," I say. Slowly, Claire creaks into a sitting position. The only chair in the room scrapes across the floor as I pull it over next to her. Rotating the table that's beside her bed, I position it so it's suspended over her legs.

"Oh blast. I almost forgot." Walking across the small room, I disappear into its bathroom to find a towel.

"This is the biggest one I could find." I carefully tuck the towel under Claire's chin. It billows around her like Superman's cape.

"Okay. Boy, dinner sure looks good tonight." Sitting on the chair next to her bed, I spoon the colourless hospital food into her mouth. When the first plate is finished, I push it aside and start on the second.

"Ready for dessert? I'm sure it's yummy." Claire plows through two servings of Styrofoam-like cake.

"Well done! You're all right now? I'll see you tomorrow, then." A quick kiss; then I leave the room and find a nurse at the station across the hall.

"She ate everything tonight. You'll not be pleased with me, though. I've left evidence that I've been there—the floor right beside the bed is soaking wet. Not too safe. I'm terribly sorry."

"Not to worry, Mr. Smith. I'll go right in and wipe it up." Grabbing a mop from the closet at the nursing station, she walks quickly into Claire's room to deal with the puddle.

November 1997
The Ottawa Hospital
Renée

Raw air and cutting wind describe most Novembers in Canada; their brisk weather warns of imminently approaching winters. This awful November is no different. I'm barely coping with the harsh reality of my daughter's accident, as well as with all the changes that are only just beginning to force themselves on all our lives.

Daily, I push Claire in her wheelchair on endlessly long excursions outdoors around the colorless, uninspiring grounds of the Ottawa Hospital. The lawns are now carpeted with dying brown grass and crisp leaves from the sleeping trees. When December inevitably arrives and winter settles in, the air is even more frigid. Snow soon drapes over the dull brown lawns and nestles on the wooden benches standing along the paved paths. Although it's cold enough on some days that slippery ice coats these walkways, the weather does not stop me.

"Okay, let's get you ready." To prepare Claire for a trek, I first dress her warmly. To ward off the increasingly wintery weather outside, I wrap her up in a ski jacket, pull a hat down over her ears, snuggle a scarf around her neck and cover her hands with warm mittens. Warm winter boots soon cuddle Claire's feet. Finally, I tuck a thin hospital blanket around her.

"The wind is really cold today. Let me see if I can get that scarf a little higher." I tug the scarf up as far as I can. Although I'm sure that I have clipped the world as she sees it, that it's now truncated sharply along the bottom like a bad haircut, I don't care. I want to shield her from the winter weather as much I can.

Steering Claire in her wheelchair out of her room, I stop at the nursing station.

"Whose turn is it today?" Lately I've been coercing one of the nurses to go with us. Claire's getting a lot stronger; sometimes I just can't persuade her to stay in the chair. My endless reading of anything that relates to her injury warns that wandering behavior can occur during post-traumatic amnesia. Her behavior seems to be following the predictions, so I make sure that I have someone along to help me deal with Claire's propensity to explore her surroundings. Being an athlete, she's very strong. Occasionally she throws the light blue synthetic blanket onto the snow and leaps out of the chair. She then weaves purposefully through the snow toward the hospital's faceless walls and pounds on locked windowless doors—some of which are marked Danger—for which only the maintenance staff has keys.

It's startling, to say the least, when she does this because it's totally uncharacteristic. The Claire I knew before the accident was always so composed, so in control of herself. Even though I intellectually know that she's exhibiting classic PTA symptoms, her actions have given me even more cause to worry. *Where is she? This is not the daughter I know so well.*

As we wheel out through the main entrance, a blast of winter air assaults us. The nurse shivers, perhaps regretting her decision to come along with us. "Lord love you for taking Claire out these days," she says to me.

"I know it's cold out, but Claire needs to realize that there's more to life than the interior of this hospital." By taking her on these outings, I'm trying—hoping—to show her that the world is composed of more than what she is exposed to most of the time, the antiseptic inner walls of the building.

Without these walks, the staff would have their hands full because I'm adamant that Claire be given no drugs. If the nurses could keep her quiet by sedating her, it would mean much less work for them. But I'm successful in my attempt to stop doctors from medicating Claire. My parental instincts have been in overdrive since the accident. By "exercising" Claire, I'm able to avoid what I feel would be yet another attack on her body, in the form of medications that I'm convinced are unnecessary. She's so much better; she's walking and talking now. I don't want them to shut her down by medicating her.

One day, I bring Splash, our enormous golden retriever, in for a visit. Everyone hopes that my daughter will know him; he's a regular part of life around the farm at home. At around two o'clock on Thursday afternoon, Splash nudges open the door of Claire's room. "Splash! You brought Splash!" To my amazement, Claire gets off the bed and, without turning toward me, lifts the huge dog up onto her bed. Her ability to do so floors me—he must weigh over 90 pounds. Splash turns his wide golden retriever head to look at me. At first he seems embarrassed; his eyes plead with me as if to say, "It's not my fault!" But he makes himself comfortable on the bed and soon appears to be very pleased with himself, delighted to be the guest of honour.

"Splash! Get down!" I say. Splash pointedly ignores me. He settles in, his deep brown eyes assuring me that everything is fine, although we both know that it's not really. At home, he wouldn't even consider jumping up on furniture.

"Splash! Do you hear me?" Oh dear, I sound just like my husband. His kids grown up, Brad sometimes seems desperate for something to control, someone who will listen to him. His authoritative voice is, however, usually met by a friendly, drooling golden retriever wagging its tail. As mine is, his attempts at control are always futile.

Claire scrabbles off the bed, weaves toward me and takes Splash's leash out of my hand, clipping it on his collar.

"Where are you going?" I ask as Claire and Splash head out the doorway.

"Visiting."

Grabbing the door frame to balance herself, Claire then lurches down the hallway, swaying from side to side. A nurse walks toward her.

"Claire! Who's your friend?"

"Splash," she informs the nurse. "We're going for a walk".

The two of them slowly make their way down the hall. Led by Claire, Splash nudges into each room so she can introduce that wonderful dog to everyone who is part of her new world: doctors, nurses, therapists and other patients.

After an hour, it's time for Splash and me to leave.

"No, no, no! Leave him here." Claire clutches his collar and hugs him tightly.

"You're coming home for the weekend tomorrow. You'll see him then." We try to bring Claire home most weekends. Splash and I walk out of Claire's room. But Claire is firmly in the present. By the time that my daughter sees him again the next day, she will have completely forgotten that the dog was in to visit her just the day before.

Late December 1997
Burritt Farm
Renée

Brad and I take Claire home for the holidays so that we can spend Christmas as a family. Claire's brothers are home too; we all try to make the day extra special, in hopes that if we do, she might—just might—remember. But I soon realize that for her December 25 just came and then vanished, as time has since September 13.

However, although her contiguous memory has not returned, Brad and I—hopefully—think that she shows some improvement in other areas. This may have been because of the familiar surroundings of home. We decide to keep her home a bit longer.

Claire's still at home with us when, during the early days of January 1998, Eastern Canada is struck by a mammoth ice storm. The crippling storm abruptly makes basic living very complicated for a lot of people. Over the course of five days, accumulating ice causes millions of dollars' worth of damage. Steel towers and hydro poles collapse. The weight of the ice damages or destroys many trees. There are massive hydro outages, and some areas are without electricity for weeks. About 35 people die.

Although power is restored in only a couple of days in downtown Ottawa, the hydro in the country near where we live is out for over two weeks. Brad and I wage a constant battle against the natural disaster that has crippled our farm. The ordeal causes us enormous amounts of work and forces us to assume a pioneering lifestyle. It's a far cry from what is our normal reality.

The Lost Months

The four months immediately following the accident will never exist for me. During those months, post-traumatic amnesia (PTA) was hard at work, successfully preventing me from storing memories of new experiences. Traditionally described as the inability to lay down memories reliably from one day to the next,[12] more recently post-traumatic amnesia has had its definition broadened to include a confused sense of time, place and person. Longer durations of PTA are associated with more severe brain injuries, lengthier hospitalizations and longer recovery times. PTA duration is one measure used to predict how well a person will function following a brain injury.[1314] The length of time I lived with PTA falls into the "very severe" head injury categorization.

I have no memory of the trip in the air ambulance that took me from the competition site to Queen's Medical Centre in Nottingham, England. I don't remember the time at that hospital. I don't remember the flight home to Canada six weeks after the accident. I don't remember being a patient at the Ottawa Hospital until Christmas. I don't remember Christmas or the first couple of weeks of January 1998. From September 13, 1997, until the middle of January 1998, I lived in the moment, under the spell of PTA.

I'll never have any memories from those mystical, imaginary months. It's become what I call my "in-between time," time that was real for everyone around me but just didn't exist for me. During those in-between months, my world consisted of only the current moment. I was told many times what had happened: "You've fallen from Gordon," but during the 16 weeks immediately following the accident, I couldn't retain any new knowledge that would normally become memory.

The last thing I remember doing is jumping the second fence on the cross-country course 30 seconds before I fell. Any "memories" that I have of my ride after the second fence and of the fall itself are imaginative and creative constructions pieced together from others' stories of that terrible day. In the early years after my fall, the curtains of my mind would occasionally part briefly to reveal a fleeting memory of something that had happened during the in-between time. However, the curtains always quickly drew shut again, rehiding the memory so that it retreated, vanishing almost as suddenly as it had appeared. I was always left wondering whether the flash of memory—sometimes it was just a quick image of one of the doctors—was real or imagined. For the past several years, the curtains have remained closed, so I haven't experienced any more random, minute flashbacks from that vanished time.

As frightening as PTA sounds, I now know that it would have been incredibly more difficult to deal with the interminable hospital stays and the drastic changes to my lifestyle necessitated by the fall *without* the cushioning and limited awareness brought about by the amnesia. It made time stand still. Nevertheless, I feel quietly alarmed when I'm told stories about what happened during that in-between time. During those 16 weeks, I had no idea of who I had been, what had happened, where I was or why I was there. I remembered nothing and lived only in the current moment.

The in-between-ness of those four months will always swirl around inside me—the lost months of post-traumatic amnesia will forever be untethered, loose, without the solid base of evolving time. Because the memories that I normally would have accumulated were never formed, I'm blissfully unaware of the missing memories contained within those months.

RESTITUTION

The plot of the restitution [narrative] has the basic storyline:
"Yesterday I was healthy, today I'm sick, but
tomorrow I'll be healthy again."[15]

Reawakening

January 15, 1998
Burritts Rapids

Late in the afternoon, I woke up in my childhood bedroom at my parent's house. The air was bracingly cold in my room. *Strange.* I swung my feet out of bed, touching them down on the old pine floor. *Yikes*—it was freezing! My next step landed on the rug, so although the air was still frigid, my feet quickly recovered from their shock. I made my way unsteadily across the room, the old wooden door creaking as I pulled it open, alerting everyone that I was awake. I would have liked to go downstairs, but first I would have had to climb over my father. He was lying on the floor outside my room, blocking the entrance to the steep stairway of the old stone house. I wondered why he was resting in such a strange place. Without moving, Cruddums mumbled: "Go back to bed." It didn't occur to me to question him, so I turned around and made my way back into my room.

After four months of nothingness, that event marked the moment when I slowly began to peek out from under the dark curtain of post-traumatic amnesia. That memory of January 15, 1997, waking up at home and finding my father lying outside my bedroom door, has stayed with me, but all other memories of the ice storm have vanished.

From that point on, I started to string together memories, right up to the moment that Gordon and I were jumping the second fence on the course at Burghley. I remembered odd things, like the fact that Kim had led Gordon in a counter-clockwise circle in the small start box, and that, to boost my own confidence, I had reached back with my crop and used it lightly behind my left leg while jumping the second fence.

At home on my parents' farm, there was no power for a few days before my memory started to return and then for at least two more weeks. The power outage meant that my mother had to cook everything in a huge iron cauldron suspended from an old iron rod over the fireplace in the kitchen. The cauldron had been hung years before when they bought the property because it was authentic and decorative. She'd never used the huge pot, but now it was a godsend. Mom cooked all of our meals in it, and the fireplace around it was one of two providing the only source of heat. My parents were constantly adding wood to keep both burning.

It looked magical outside. The world glistened; ice coated everything, brazenly reflecting the sunlight. However, it viciously contrasted with our dark existence without hydro. In the kitchen, the natural light coming in through the two small windows wasn't much help in illuminating the low-ceilinged room. There was only one other source of light, the kitchen fire. As the firelight danced across Mom and Dad's faces, I was oblivious to the fact that it revealed worry lines that etched more deeply as each day passed without electricity. But as my PTA had only just started to recede, I was completely unaware of the harsh reality of my parents' daily lives.

Mom and Cruddums slouched in their chairs in the kitchen on a Sunday morning during the ice storm, but I was bouncing around the table. I didn't understand why my parents didn't seem to have any energy.

"What are we going to do today?" I asked brightly, impatiently waiting for their reply.

"What would you like to do?" my mother replied, draining the last drop of coffee from the pot. Painstakingly made over the open fire, it was liquid gold.

Sounding just like a young child, I announced, "I really want to go outside."

"Okay, wait for a bit, and then one of us will take you out. Darling, if I stay here with Claire, can you manage a few trips down the hill to get water for the cows"? Mom asked Cruddums.

Cruddums took a deep breath and slowly eased out of this chair, unfolding his body with great care. I wondered why he was so creaky.

"Why are you so stiff? Maybe it's because you're not running these days."

"I've been carrying heavy buckets up from the river instead! Okay, I'll go and get ready." Cruddums slowly made his way toward the mudroom and prepared himself for the ice-covered world outside.

The river, which lay at the bottom of the hill behind the house, was the only source of water for the animals. Growing up, we had flown down the hill on toboggans and crazy carpets, often crashing into the snow fence my father put up each winter to stop us from sliding onto the river ice. Although it was treasured in the summer as a place to relax and cool down, during the ice storm the river became associated with the back-breaking chore of hauling water for the cattle. My parents were physically exhausted from their endless trips up and down the hill.

There was so much to do just to keep the pipes from freezing, us fed, and the cows fed and watered. No generators were available in Ottawa; all models had been sold soon after the hydro failed. One of my brothers, who lived in New York City, bought a generator there and drove it up to the farm. Between filling it with fuel every few hours and keeping the fireplaces going, my father got little sleep.

I was the extra work that no one needed. It was essential that there was always someone with me when I was outside. I needed to be watched carefully when I wandered around; I moved quickly on the extremely slippery ice. No one knew where I would meander next, where I was headed or why I was headed in that direction. I wore a helmet because the ice that coated everything often broke loose from trees and buildings.

At two o'clock in the afternoon, I looked out the window from my position in front of the fireplace and saw the sunshine gleaming off the iced-covered trees. The shiny world outside beckoned.

"Can we go outside now?"

Mom sighed, breathing in deeply before she replied, "Sure, let's get you dressed."

My mother closed her eyes for a just second. I followed her from the family room, now heated only by the fireplace, into the cold mudroom. As I walked through the doorway separating the two, I left the door open. Mom's shoulders dropped. She didn't bother saying anything, but she reached around behind me to shut the door. I sat on the bench in the mudroom, and she got me all bundled up.

"Here, be still."

"Mom! I don't need to wear one," I protested as she slid a snowmobile helmet onto my head. "These are for old people. I'll be fine. Really!" She ignored me and proceeded to buckle crampons to my boots.

"There, you're all set!" We headed out the door into the glistening world. As I always did, I wove unsteadily toward the barn. Only five minutes later, Mom frantically slithered down the frozen driveway toward me. A huge slab of ice had just let go from the peak of the barn roof. Sliding down the length of the roof, it splintered loudly when it crashed onto the ice-covered ground.

"Brad! Watch her! Claire! I need you to stay away from the buildings! Please! Thank God you're wearing a helmet. I have no idea if it would really help, but it soothes my frayed nerves just a little."

My mother and father were both desperately clinging to the prognosis made by the neurologists in England: "In a year, you won't know that anything has happened to her." But, while my father stoically soldiered on, my mother was in despair. Surrounded by her emotional pain and overcome by it all, she was really depressed about what she'd read on head injury; she was not at all convinced that I would ever bear any resemblance to the old me.

My parents realized that I seemed to remember everything that had happened since about the middle of January. But, although the doctors' predictions seemed confident, and although they had no alternative but to believe the doctors, my parents remained very concerned. It had already been about four months since my accident, but I was still functioning like a young child. Curious about everything, I was learning about and exploring the world around me. I expected—even wanted—my parents to tell me what to do, and I had no clue that I'd ever had the crucial life skills of planning and decision-making. I was thinking in very concrete and immediate terms, so I felt ready to be who I'd been before, ready to take up where I had left off. For me, my future was a forgone conclusion, but for my parents it remained very unsure.

The heavy veil of PTA was gradually lifting from my life when Mom and Dad had a talk with me in the kitchen one Saturday evening in late January. The candles cast an inconsistent light on the kitchen table; the flickering light seemed to turn quickly into shadows when I thought about my horses. But Mom and Cruddums were hoping that, at least for the time being, I would focus on rehabilitation and less on my past life, so they made a big deal over it now being time for the next stage of my recovery. The next day, Mom was going to take me to a hospital. She explained that the therapists there could help me get better, but she didn't say how long I would be staying. Although they carefully told me where I was going and why I was going there, I had only recently been able to access my memories, so I couldn't draw any images of a hospital in my mind. My parents emphasized that I would have to try hard and do all the exercises that the therapists gave me as homework. It sounded to me as if it would be just like school.

Another Hospital

Sunday night, February 15, 1998
Saint-Vincent Hospital, Ottawa

At about five o'clock the next afternoon, my mother and I got into the car. Butterflies fluttered in my stomach. I had not felt any since I cantered down the centreline in the dressage test at Burghley, England, in September 1997, the day before I fell. I didn't know what to expect from this next chapter of rehabilitation. Cruddums kissed me on the cheek.

"Think of it as a big adventure. I'll see you tomorrow. We'll go for a walk and explore the neighbourhood."

The winter night was fast approaching; what daylight remained faded rapidly from the January sky as Mom drove toward the city, about 45 minutes away. She turned left into a residential area before she reached downtown; soon the streets became smaller and smaller. I blew hot air on the passenger-side window, melting the frost so I could peek at the neighbourhood outside. We turned left at the four-way stop, then right and right again. I saw that the houses were getting smaller and rougher. When we turned left up a short incline, there was suddenly a red brick wall, about eight stories high, looming right in front of me.

"We're here!"

Mom parked the car in front of what looked like the main entrance: grey metal doors, each with a window, and a single light shining overhead. My view was disappearing, so I blew more air on the car window. I was appalled by what I saw, a dismal old building that looked desperately in need of a renovation. Mom turned off the car, looked in the rear-view mirror at her reflection and sighed. She'd gotten a lot greyer, and there were bags under her eyes. I kept my mouth shut, but I could have told her she didn't look great. Unbuckling our seat belts, we got out of the car.

"Careful, it might be slippery. Can you reach into the back seat and get the bag?"

Inside, it was as cold and grey as the January weather outside. The long hallway before us had probably been white years ago, but it was now desperately in need of a fresh coat of paint. When we reached the end of the uninspiring hall, we pulled open a door that led into a stairwell. Our echoing footsteps loudly announced our presence to all as we trudged up the uncarpeted steps to the brain injury rehabilitation unit on the second floor.

The unit's entrance was not far along yet another bare corridor. We opened the single metal door; then we heard the door closing softly behind us and clicking firmly shut as it locked us in the ward.

A bad omen. It seems that you can't leave this place.

The long, dreary hallway led to a nurse sitting behind a desk.

"Hi, you must be Claire," she said, glancing at the notebook in front of her. "I'm Cathy. I'll show you where you'll be staying while you're here."

Cathy came out from behind the desk and walked into the room right across the hall. The utilitarian room had two single beds. A TV hung from the wall at the foot of each bed. There was a window, its curtains pulled shut to hide the darkness outside.

"Sharon will be your roommate."

In the bed closer to the window lay an older woman, who raised her right hand and waved weakly at us.

Oh, great. There's obviously lots of excitement in this room.

Opposite Sharon's bed, a narrow doorway led to a small bathroom with a toilet and a sink.

"Sharon, I'm just going to show Claire and her mother where the showers are. We'll be right back." Cathy led us down the hall; she pulled open a door and walked into a unisex washroom. Facing us were four shower stalls, each one with its own tiny change room. To the right was a row of four toilet stalls.

We walked back to the room I was to share with Sharon. "Well, that's all you'll need to know before the morning. In the meantime, if you need me, I'm right across the hall from your room."

I clutched my gym bag just like a small child holding a teddy bear. "Here, pass me that bag, and I'll unpack it for you," Mom said. Slouched on the narrow bed, I watched as Mom took a week's worth of my clothes from the gym bag and put it away in the narrow closet.

"There. You all right? I'll come by tomorrow."

She wrapped her arms around me and hugged me. When I started to cry, pleading with Mom not to leave me, she hesitated for a few seconds and wiped her eyes. Wavering, indecision written all over her face, she finally marched resolutely down the hall, leaving me, a sobbing heap of daughter, collapsed on the bed.

Cathy popped her head into the room.

"Honey, she's coming to see you tomorrow. Here, let me show you how the TV works."

I was easily distracted, so when she gave me the remote, I flipped through the channels, settling on a game show. I stopped crying, and Cathy left the room.

"You're up early," said the nurse sitting at the desk across the hall from my room; she was not Cathy from the night before.

"It's only seven, so I've just started my shift. Did you get here last night? Let me check my notes. I'm Julie, by the way." She flipped through a binder in front of her with her right hand; her left held a Styrofoam cup of coffee. Locating my name in the binder, she said, "Oh, here you are. You must be Claire. I see it's your first day."

I told her that I was going to go and take a shower.

"Have you got a towel? Would you like me to show you how everything works?"

Is she serious? I've been taking showers for years. I was getting frustrated with how everyone, my parents included, was treating me. As far as I was concerned, I had recovered from the fall, but Mom and Dad insisted on taking all these ridiculous precautions. Dressing me in a snowmobile helmet and crampons outdoors—really! Now they'd brought me to yet another hospital, and the nurse seemed worried that I would not be able to figure out how the shower worked!

I assured her I was fine. But it was a good thing she'd asked about the towel because I'd left mine behind. Going back into my room, I found a small, almost threadbare, towel hanging next to the sink in the tiny toilet room.

"Okay. Well, if you have any questions, you know where to find me."

I made my way down the hall toward the bathroom. Choosing the nearest shower stall, I pulled the shower curtain closed behind me, its rings clattering along the metal rod. There was a bench inside the tiny space and a couple of hooks mounted on the wall. Then there was another shower curtain pushed to one side. The shower head was on the wall ahead of me, the controls directly below it. Simple. But when I turned on the shower, a blast of cold water shot across the space, soaking my pyjamas.

"Honey, figure out how it all works? Can I come in"? Julie poked her head around the corner.

"Oh dear, I guess not. Here, let me show you." She explained that I should strip first, hang my clothes on the hooks, draw the inner curtain shut and then push it aside just enough to be able reach in and turn on the shower.

"See, then your clothes won't get all wet. Be patient; it sometimes takes a minute before the hot water gets here. Don't forget to turn the shower off before you open the curtain; otherwise your clothes will get even wetter."

I guess most of the people here have to have it all laid out for them, step by step. But I would have figured it out myself, no problem. It's obvious that they're not used to patients who are as well as I am.

When I finished my shower and went back to the depressing room I was sharing with Sharon, there was a lady I didn't know sitting in a chair next to my bed.

"Hi, Claire. I'm Susie. I'll be with you for the rest of the day. I see that you've already taken a shower." Her eyes took in my sodden PJs. "Give me those when you've changed, and I'll make sure they get put in the dryer."

I went into the tiny bathroom and changed, handing the dripping PJs to Susie when I reappeared. Just then an orderly came into the room with breakfast. Slouching on the bed, I was not at all inspired when I looked it over: buttered toast that I was sure would be cold, dry cereal with a glass of milk beside it, a glass of orange juice and a banana too ripe to eat.

"Dear, we'll go to your appointment, physiotherapy, in 20 minutes, so work on that breakfast," said Susie. I wondered whether I should offer the breakfast to her because my stomach churned at the thought of eating any of it. And I was not her "dear"! My dark mood was not improved when I looked out the window; a nurse must have drawn open its dark beige curtains. All I could see was the dull grey wall of the next building.

"Are you sure you're not hungry? You won't have anything until lunch if you don't eat," Susie said, sitting on the chair beside my bed, a bright pink acrylic sweater several sizes too small stretched across her ample bosom.

My smile didn't spread to my eyes. *She must think I'm stupid! Of course I know that. She can have the breakfast if she wants. I don't want any of it.*

At nine o'clock every morning, I went to physiotherapy. It soon became my favourite time of the day—I could move! In a room at the end of the hall, I rode a stationary bike and did other exercises. Every morning, about 15 minutes after I got there, a young male patient was lifted into the room. His body was a mess; he was transported in a huge sling. I marvel now at the creativity and inventiveness of the physiotherapists who had to design rehabilitation for him and for other patients with catastrophic physical injuries. At the time, however, I was oblivious to the world around me.

When Cruddums came by at lunchtime that first day, I asked him about Susie. He told me that she was there to keep me company. Only much later did I realize that this was only partially true. The real reason was that the hospital's nurses just did not have enough time to watch me as carefully as was necessary, so my parents had hired sitters to be with me during the day. This was especially important at mealtimes because I had no appetite for the uninspiring hospital food. Although Susie tried a couple more times that first morning to persuade me to eat, my breakfast remained untouched. Every morning, the breakfast looked the same, and every morning I refused to eat it. Most days I wouldn't touch much of lunch or dinner, either. There were other sitters too. I got to know what day it was by the sitter who was with me: Susie on Mondays, Cathy on Tuesdays, Precious on Wednesdays and June on Thursdays. I never knew who would be there on Fridays. Not one of them had much luck trying to get me to eat.

No one was sure that I would not get lost within the hospital, so it was arranged for me to have a hospital porter take me to the various therapies.

"Are you ready to go?" asked the man who walked briskly into my room after physio on that first Monday morning.

"I'm Jacques. I'll take you to your appointment with Dr. Bell, the speech therapist. All set?" I was going to see the speech therapist because my parents thought that my speech was still thick and that I was slurring my words. Personally, I felt that they just couldn't stop worrying about me. I felt I'd recovered, but they were having trouble letting me go.

I followed Jacques out the door of my room. When we got to the locked door at the end of the hall, he waved a pass at it, pulled it open and walked through.

"Hey, where did you get that? I want one too! I'm locked up like a dangerous animal in here."

"I'll be going to all your appointments with you, so you don't need one."

"Have you had a head injury too?" At first, I didn't understand what he meant.

Jacques laughed. "No, I'm here to help you transition to regular life." He got it! He seemed to know that being incarcerated in this hospital was far from the way I was used to living.

"I'll go with you to your therapies, and then, in a few weeks, you'll be able to find your own way."

A few weeks! Does he think I'm an idiot? This hospital is ridiculous. Wait till I tell Mom and Dad. They obviously don't know that everyone is treating me like a small child.

Although there was no way I would have admitted it, Jacques was right. For the first couple of weeks, he led me through beige corridors that all looked the same. I saw lots of grey metal doors and echoing stairwells. The single elevator was always very crowded. I walked through overflowing wards in which some patients were lying on cots in the hall. When I started to know my way around, I led Jacques, not the other way around. He was careful, walking close behind me at first and then gradually giving me more freedom. Near the end of my stay, I was buzzed through the locked door at the end of the hall and went by myself to the therapists' offices. I felt trusted: I was finally free of the constant supervision that I had been under since my fall. I'm now sure that the nurses responsible for me kept a close eye. There was no doubt some system they had for checking on my arrival at my destination within the hospital.

One, or sometimes both, of my parents came to the hospital most days. My father and I went for walks around the neighbourhood by the hospital when he visited me during his daily lunch breaks.

Sitting on my bed, I pulled on my boots and shrugged into my jacket.

"Where's your scarf?" asked Cruddums; he was rarely without one himself. I rolled my eyes, but before I zipped the jacket all the way up, I wrapped a scarf around my bare neck, snugly covering it. Then I reached into my jacket pockets and found my sheepskin mittens.

"Are we off? Here, make sure your wrists are covered. It's really cold out." He pulled each mitten up until it overlapped my jacket.

Once outside, I shielded my eyes from the midday sun. It bounced harshly off the snow and straight into my eyes, which were now accustomed to indoor light. I was glad that Cruddums had insisted on a scarf; it was freezing out.

"I've got your sunglasses." Cruddums handed them to me; he kept the glasses between our outings.

What is his problem? I'm old enough to look after my own glasses.

"Let's try going down the street away from downtown." Cruddums took my arm. He did so whenever it might be the least bit slippery, although all the sidewalks had been thoroughly salted. I immediately shook free of his grasp. A Walk signal flashed on the other side of the street we were going to cross. I knew what he'd say next.

"Now, what should you do?"

I rolled my eyes and recited the expected answer: "We can walk when there's a signal, but first I need to check for cars that are turning onto the street I'm crossing, cars that have a green light. They are supposed to let me cross before they turn, but I need to assume that anyone driving is an idiot."

"Good for you!"

How old does he think I am, anyway? Cruddums continued to review all the basics I'd ever been taught: to look both ways before crossing the street, not to walk right next to the curb, it was safer to be as far as possible away from it. To be aware of cars turning right, into the crosswalk, when their light was green. We walked for about half an hour.

"Okay, it's time to head back." We turned toward the hospital, but the lesson continued. I hoped that no one knew me.

When we got back to my room, I waved to Sharon and pulled off my outdoor clothing. Cruddums draped my coat over the one chair in the room so any damp spots would dry. He put my sunglasses into their case and slid it into the breast pocket of his winter jacket. My cheeks were rosy as I hugged him goodbye.

"See you at the same time tomorrow." Waving, he strode off down the hall.

On the weekends, I always insisted that we visit my horses. They were still at the stable where the owner had offered to take them when I was first injured. One freezing-cold day early in February, Mom made sure that I was well bundled up before we left home. Once at the barn, she snapped several photos of Gordon and me standing in the snow. Then, using the best photo, she made cards, which she sent to all the people who had called, sent cards, or come to visit. Soon after that, Gordon was shipped to North Carolina, so Mike could ride him.

Years later, I find it fascinating that, when Sunday afternoon came around, I never minded going back to the hospital. I suppose I thrived on the routine there, and I think I unconsciously knew that the therapists were helping me to get better. When she brought me back each week, my mother, having taken a week's worth of my clothes home on Friday to wash, hung clothes in the small closet for me to wear during the coming week. I waved goodbye and settled in.

The archaic surroundings gave no indication of the helpful services provided within. Despite myself, I almost enjoyed the three months that I was a patient at Saint-Vincent's. I think that, just like affection and human touch make babies feel secure and loved, I felt protected and safe. I was looked after and not required to make any decisions. The staff and therapists were kind, and they did their best to help me in any way they could. As well as physiotherapy, I had speech therapy, occupational therapy and sessions with a psychiatrist.

By the beginning of March, I was growing impatient with the hospital and its restrictions on me. I was easily making my way around by myself; Jacques the porter no longer followed me. I felt ready to try something else new, to test my growing capabilities. I had a dentist's appointment the following week, with Dr. Earle, who had been my family's dentist for years. His office was in an old brick office building that had once been a large house; it was only a few blocks from downtown. Cruddums picked me up and drove me to my appointment. But rather than sitting and waiting for me, he gave me a longer leash, telling me to walk to his office when the appointment was over. I was to make my way to the end of the dentist's street when I was finished, which met the large street leading to his office.

"Are you sure you're going to be all right? Remember, it's left out the door, then left on Bank Street when you reach the traffic lights."

Is he ever going to relax?

Cruddums glanced nervously at the secretary. "Okay, I'll just wait here until they come to get you." He settled into a chair. The office is very punctual, so just when he was comfortably seated and was about to flip through a magazine, one of the assistants came to the door of the waiting room.

"Claire? Come with me, please."

"Okay, well, I guess it's your turn. Are you going to be all right?" He'd started to sound like a broken record.

"Fine, Dad. I'll be just fine!"

"Remember we practised during our walks at lunchtime?" Actually, I was wondering whether I would ever be able to forget those embarrassing walks. Cruddums gave me a quick hug and was gone.

After the appointment, I walked out the door of the dentist's office, down the short flight of steps to the street and then along the sidewalk for a block until I reached the larger street. When there was a Walk signal, I crossed the street and then turned left to make my way toward Cruddums' office. The exercise was harder than I'd expected. I concentrated on crossing intersecting streets only when there was a Walk signal and walking close to the buildings, not to the road.

I wasn't sure what to do when someone walked straight toward me. Should I move over? What if I had to move too close to the busy street? Several times I found myself facing another pedestrian. I wanted to tell the person to move out of the way, but I didn't, so we played this silly left, right, left again game. Finally it was clear ahead of me as well as clear beside me for the other person. Triumphantly, I saw that I wasn't too near the curb. Yay for me! I saw my father several blocks away, pacing nervously outside his building.

"So how was it?" I felt that I should be asking him that. Cruddums looked relieved.

"You want a coffee? I'll get you one on the way to the car. I'm sure you want to celebrate." He gave me a hug.

"I'm fine! It was no problem." We celebrated with a coffee, and then he drove me back to the hospital.

The following week, Mike came for a couple of days and stayed at a bed and breakfast near the hospital. He had phoned me every night while I was a patient, talking with me about my horses and keeping me up to date on what was happening in Southern Pines. The nightly calls and their conversations were yet another attempt by me, albeit unconscious at the time, to cling to the person I had been before the accident. When Mike visited, it was early in March, about a month before I was to be discharged. We went out for dinner and talked more about how my horses were doing. I wanted to know what was happening in North Carolina. He was competing Gordon, who had been shipped to North Carolina for him to ride in late January. I couldn't wait to move back down.

Many years elapsed before I was emotionally distanced enough from the turmoil surrounding the accident to understand how shattered Mike had been by my fall. He'd been involved in a high-risk sport for years, but never before had he been personally affected; no one close to him had been so seriously injured. He flew to England to see me when I was still in the hospital in Nottingham. My parents were making educated and informed decisions concerning my care in Canada once I was ready to be flown home, but Mike's emotions guided his thoughts about what would be best for me. He insisted that I go to the United States to receive the best medical care, but his opinion was not based on any research that he had done.

Mike's desperation made an already tense association with my parents that much worse; they had never approved of our relationship. As is typical when a child is seriously hurt, my parents huddled around me and pushed others, in this case Mike, away. They didn't feel he was helping the terrible situation. Although he desperately wanted to be part of my support team, when he tried to become involved in decisions regarding my rehabilitation, both in England and at home, he was rebuffed.

March 1998
Southern Pines, North Carolina

A couple of weeks later, while I was still a patient at the hospital, I flew down to Southern Pines to see Mike and the horses of mine that were in his stable. I didn't realize, of course, that my parents were nervous about the trip. Since it was only six months after I had fallen, they knew that it would be a big test of my ability to be independent. At the same time, I was assuming that I'd soon be moving back there because my life, of course, had not changed.

I stayed with Mike and followed him everywhere; my safety and care rested on his shoulders. There'd been an unspoken shifting of roles, but I was completely unaware of how our relationship had changed. Since the accident, I'd become accustomed to always having someone to look after me. Before that I had been very independent; I would quickly have been driven crazy by someone constantly hovering around me.

I watched Mike ride Gordon at the annual horse trials in Southern Pines, which Gordon and I had won the previous year.

Gordon and Mike were in the warm-up area. They had about 15 minutes before their start time for the cross-country phase.

"Is there anything that you want me to do"? I asked.

"No, I've got a girl to help me. Why don't you go and watch."

I started walking alongside the course, past the first three straightforward fences. When I got to the combination at four, quite a lot of people were waiting to watch the next horse. It was a good place to watch because the combination was right beside the water jump, obstacle 21, negotiated on the way home. You could see two difficult obstacles from the same location. After the water, there were only two more jumps on the course.

"Much action here?" I asked a girl from the area.

"Everything is riding pretty smoothly. Some are having trouble keeping their line at the water jump, so they slip by the last element."

I heard the announcer over the loudspeaker: "Number 15, Gordon

Gibbons, ridden by eight-time Olympian Mike Plumb, is over one and two."

Unable to stand still, I hopped from one foot to the other.

There was a hush as the crowd focused on Gordon, whose ears were pricked as he glided toward the fourth combination. Jump one, two strides, jump two at an angle, three strides, out over jump three. No problem at all. Gord galloped away down the track, out of sight for five minutes.

Five minutes seemed interminable, but at least I could follow their progress by listening to the announcer. Finally, Gord and Mike reappeared in the distance. I could barely make them out as they jumped a fence far away from where I was standing, but soon they were galloping toward the water. The crowd grew quiet.

Gord's eyes were focused on what he was about to do. He leapt over the barrels—one, two, three strides—and then he jumped down into the water. Although it was only six inches deep, the water splashed everywhere. As soon as he landed, Gord immediately zeroed in on the jump out of the water, the next part of the obstacle.

My boys jumped quickly and efficiently out of the shallow water and then bounced over the narrow logs before heading home.

Ever confident, Mike knew I was there, so he waved as he galloped away.

I know what I was thinking while I was watching that day—I would be the one competing Gordon the following year. I firmly believed that it was only a matter of time before I'd resume the life I'd been living before the accident. Both the doctors and my parents were leery of my plans. When I told them that I planned on living my life as I'd always done, they were, to put it bluntly, appalled. However, any advice they tried to give me fell on deaf ears. I was convinced that things would be just as they had been. I wonder now how I would have reacted if I'd listened to what the doctors were telling me, if I'd realized that I'd have no choice but to swerve off the life path that I had chosen so many years ago.

For the first 18 months or so after PTA had retreated, from the middle of January 1998 to the summer of 1999, I was adamant that

I was going to continue living life exactly as I had been. I couldn't imagine living any other way. The doctor had told me I was doing fine, so I knew that I would soon be returning to the life I loved. Life would, of course, be the same.

I flew back to Ottawa after a week in Southern Pines. I went back to the hospital, but they couldn't do much more for me there in terms of rehabilitation, so they were going to release me. I was at the stage where I could operate on my own to a certain extent, but I needed guidance with many things that most people would find straightforward. I didn't have a driver's licence. But I was keen to get on with it, convinced that my recovery was complete. At the end of the month I was discharged, and I went home to my parents' farm.

About 10 days later, early that April, I had an appointment with the rehabilitation doctor at the hospital.

"Hi, Claire! I see it's only been a week since you went home." The doctor looked at her notes in my file.

Everyone has notes, it seems. Maybe I'll get some too. I'll fit right in, I thought uncharitably.

"I'm just going to chat with you, see how you're doing, but I'd like you to remember these three words: car, house, balloon. I'll ask you what they are before you leave."

There were about 10 minutes of the usual questions:

"How are you feeling?"

"Fine."

"Do you have any plans?"

"Yes, going to Southern Pines as soon as possible," and so on. On and on and on …

When the doctor looked at her watch, I knew that my time was almost up.

"Car, house, balloon," I blurted out triumphantly before she asked.

The doctor grinned. "You're doing just fine, aren't you? Make an appointment to see me again in about a year. I need you to remember one very important thing. Head injuries are often invisible. I caution you: people may not know your history of head injury. Invisible is great—but only when you're ready for it. For the time being, let people guide you and help you. You're still in the early stages of your recovery. Don't forget that."

Those words—car, house, balloon—have stayed with me. I just strung them together to form an image in my mind: a car parked in front of a house with a balloon tied to the aerial. That image, and those words, will be imprinted in my mind forever.

My injury was invisible, so why would my life not be the same as it always had been? Although I thought I was fixed because I was finally free from post-traumatic amnesia and no longer a patient in a hospital, I didn't yet understand that I was a changed person. After a head injury, it can take years before survivors become self-aware and realize that their lives must be very different. Sometimes it doesn't happen at all. I was clueless of the harsh reality that life could no longer be the same for me, and I remained oblivious to that reality for the next year or so.

However, everyone around me was all too aware that I had a lot more rehabilitation to do before I could even begin to function in the real world. My parents also needed guidance so that they could begin to understand the unfamiliar roles into which they'd been thrust. Mom and Cruddums had become caregivers of a severely head-injured adult, forced to take on responsibilities that were completely foreign to them. Before I was discharged, they visited a clinic that had been recommended by the doctor at the hospital. They spoke to its therapists, whom they liked right away.

The centre had an all-around approach: I would work with a speech therapist, and an occupational therapist would help me to relearn things that had been second nature before my injury. I would also have psychological counselling to help me come to terms with my losses. The therapists would work together, reteaching me that there were many roads to Rome, many ways to solve most problems. When searching for a solution to a problem that would be relatively easy to resolve preinjury, an individual with a head injury tends to try the same incorrect path countless times, not understanding that a different path might provide the solution. To address physical rehabilitation, the therapists worked with a neuro-physiotherapist at the big athletic centre down the road from the head-injury clinic.

After Mom and Cruddums' initial visit without me, they took me along to talk to Pierre, one of the founding directors of *The Phoenix Network*. The clinic is unobtrusively tucked into the middle of a strip mall on the eastern outer edges of Ottawa. Pierre met me when I walked into the centre with my parents.

"Hi, you must be Claire. Just ahead of you on the right is a meeting room. Let's go in there. Do you want to go around to the far side of the table with your parents? Good stuff! I'll sit on this side."

Despite Pierre's relaxed and understanding manner, I was very suspicious of the situation. As far as I was concerned, the visit was a waste of time, completely unnecessary. There was nothing wrong with me. Thank goodness I didn't say anything, because I was fuming: *I was fixed at the hospital, so why am I here? Can't Mom and Dad see that I want to get on with it? The fall was just a little blip in my life. I wonder why my parents and Pierre don't realize that obvious fact!* I was not at all open to more rehabilitation.

"What will I do here?" I asked. I was convinced that I was fine. *I'm cured, so the therapists don't need to help me. I'm ready to resume my life with my horses!*

Even though there was no question in my mind that I was okay, that riders fall off all the time, Pierre kept pushing therapy. "I know it's annoying to be here when you thought that you were through with therapy when you left the hospital," Pierre said.

My mind was full of what I wanted to say: *You're not kidding! Don't you realize that I'm hugely frustrated that I've even been brought here to talk to you? What do you know, anyway? You've never had a head injury.*

I was adamant that the therapy was not necessary, but my parents knew otherwise. My father drove me to the clinic soon after I left the hospital in early April 1998. Against my wishes, Cruddums dropped me off there for outpatient therapy, two or three days a week, until September.

I loved my weekly appointments with Avi, the neuro-physiotherapist.

My eyes were closed as I stood on a very soft mat in Avi's office. When I first did the exercise, I asked him what I was working on.

"We're working on refining your compromised proprioception. Your body is no longer sure of where it is in the world. If I take away the external references—your eyes and the firm floor—you'll be forced to (re)train your inner ears to help you balance."

A couple of weeks later, I conquered the exercise: I could stand on the mat for at least a minute without losing my balance, tipping and having to open my eyes.

"Hah! Pretty good, eh?" I was chuffed with myself. However, Avi had more tricks up his sleeve: he told me to try the exercise standing only on one leg! As the summer continued, my work with him became more and more refined.

As we often did, Avi and I kicked a soccer ball around on the lawn of the athletic centre. The tennis courts nearby were full; I heard soft thuds as balls met rackets. Exclamations of "Yes, that was good" and loud self-criticisms like "I can do better than that!" bounced through the air around us. Avi deftly guided the ball around me. I was too slow to stop him; he and the ball glided by.

"Claire, work on going sideways. Stop for a minute. Stay in one place, but bounce quickly from one foot to the other. Keep your knees bent. Stay alert. Anticipate. Good. Now do the same when you have the ball. Move from side to side *and* keep the ball moving with your feet as you do so." When we were playing soccer, he was working on my balance. I didn't realize it, though; I was having so much fun.

I slid the ball back and forth between my feet, kicking it softly left and then right.

"Oops." The ball got away from me. Loose, it travelled quickly toward the parking lot.

"Quick! Run after it! Get it before it's off the grass. If it goes onto the pavement, don't follow it"! When I reached the edge of the lawn,

I felt Avi's hand on my shoulder, preventing my carefree flight from continuing onto the road. He fetched the ball and threw it toward me.

"Good for you! Now kick it back to me. Use the inside of your foot."

Avi's use of games as therapy made the rehabilitation so much fun that the time flew by. I didn't realize until much later that Avi wasn't just having fun playing them with me. He was working on my response time, my reactions, my agility, my balance. Tremendously patient and enthusiastic, he successfully retaught me to move quickly and change direction easily as part of the process of rehabilitating my motor skills.

Same as Always

During the summer of 1998, I found a friend in Glennis, Pierre's co-director, who was my psychological counsellor at the head-injury clinic. The first time we met, Glennis assured me that our meetings were confidential; no one outside the room would know what we had discussed. We talked at length about all sorts of things, including my equestrian life. It was soon very apparent to her that, as far as I was concerned, the role of my equestrian life in my future was not even under consideration; it was still everything to me.

However, what was glaringly obvious to both Glennis and my parents was not at all evident to me. I didn't yet realize that the accident had forced enormous changes upon me. I refused to believe that horses could no longer be at the forefront of my life. With the right drugs and the right therapy, I thought, I'd surely be as good as new, able to continue life as it had been. I saw no reason why life could not be the exactly as before. I refused to even think that anything had to change, and I expected Glennis to help me resume my old life.

A little over a year after my fall, I was bound and determined to travel to Southern Pines and return to the life I was so familiar with, the only one I wanted to live. Glennis assured my concerned parents that they should let me go. Ever wise, she knew that I was going through a typical phase of recovery. I will always have the greatest respect for Glennis's counselling talents. She did not tell me forthrightly that my life would

118

have to change. She knew, from her years of experience as a counselor to survivors of head injury, that I had to discover for myself that I could no longer live my old life. I wouldn't accept that harsh reality if I were told so by others. Glennis skillfully and tactfully guided me so that I would eventually come to the realization myself.

The English poet John Keats (1795–1821) wrote that nothing becomes real until it is experienced. I needed to experience my old way of being, to attempt to live my former life, before my post-head-injury life could become my new reality. Glennis understood that unless I tried to continue my life with horses, I would forever resent being told by others that I shouldn't ride. To me, she seemed to be the one person who was on my side, and I think now that she really was on my side—in a very carefully designed way.

So, although my parents were very worried about my intentions to resume my former life, I flew down to North Carolina in November 1998.

"Why on earth is Claire down there?" I'm sure that if my father did not say those exact words to my mother, he was thinking them.

"Darling, remember that Glennis assured us that she just needs some time to realize that she can't ride and compete like she used to? Claire needs to come to that conclusion herself. If *we* tell her that her life has to change, she'll always resent us."

Finally, I was back in Southern Pines, living with Mike. My old familiar life was going to be the same as it always had been. Mike was there, my horses were there. There was no question in my mind that I was meant to be there; there was no way that my riding career could no longer be the centre of my life. Why wouldn't it be?

The first horse I rode after my fall was my old buddy, Gordon. I was still thinking like a rider and a trainer: when I first got on, Gord's trot felt different circling to the left than to the right. I immediately told Mike. He laughed and told me, "You're still the same!"

My life in North Carolina felt reassuringly familiar. To me, it was close to being as it should be. The same familiar way would go on. During the late fall of 1998, I was quite content to watch Mike ride my horses. Although I rode daily, I attended competitions only as a spectator. A week before Christmas, I flew home to Canada.

On December 20, my father and I got into the car. He drove west for almost an hour, heading farther into the countryside. I had no idea where we were going. We reached the outskirts of a small town, and Cruddums turned into the gravel driveway of a bungalow.

When we rang the front doorbell, an elderly gentleman answered, gradually easing the door open, his slippered foot guarding against an approaching sea of yellow puppies.

"Quickly, quickly now. Before they get out!"

Cruddums and I squeezed through the doorway seconds before the golden retriever mass reached the opening.

"Hi. Sorry for the overly enthusiastic welcome! I'm Larry. Around your feet is Belle's litter, seven weeks old. We've got two litters. May's are three weeks younger."

We walked down the hall toward the kitchen, which was littered with wood shavings. We dodged adorable puppies the whole way. Whiffs of disinfectant permeated the air.

"Sorry, there are shavings everywhere. This is my wife, Nancy."

From where she was sitting among the puppies, Nancy tried to stand and greet us, but the same enthusiastic committee who had welcomed Dad and me swarmed her. She gave up trying to be polite, instead lifting two of the puppies and nestling them into her lap.

"Hi. Obviously, I can't get up!"

In the kitchen, a female golden was lying on her left side, a row of eight puppies insistently nudging her belly as they suckled.

"The older litter will be ready to go in a week; they're all spoken for. Have a look at the younger litter; they'll be here for another month. Most of them are still available," Nancy told us from where she was sitting, yet more puppies on her lap.

Larry explained how puppies were placed. "We do things a little differently. Rather than you choose a puppy, we'll choose the best puppy for you because we get to know them all individually. Tell us what you're looking for, and we'll find the best match."

"Oh, they're all adorable, but I'd like to have a quiet, light-coloured female," I said.

"We'll do our best. Glad you stopped by to see them."

My father, a sucker for baby animals, was enchanted. "They're so cute. I'm tempted to take them all home now!"

As we walked down the hall toward the front door, Larry tried to herd the pack of loose puppies back into the dining room. When we got to the door, he told us to hurry: "They move so quickly that you have less than five seconds to leave! Thanks so much for dropping by. We'll chat soon."

Back in the car, I turned excitedly to my Dad. "Wow, thank you!"

On the seventh of January, I went back to Southern Pines. Mike was probably a lot less excited than I was about the arrival of Water Lily, the name I'd given the puppy, but he played the game well and enjoyed my anticipation as I waited impatiently for her arrival. My mother had booked a flight for Lily so that she could join me in North Carolina when she was eight weeks old and ready to leave her mother. It's almost always freezing cold in Canada in the middle of January, when the puppy was to fly, and the flights to Raleigh from Ottawa at that time all connected through Toronto. Mom didn't like the thought of Lily, who would be flying cargo, sitting in her crate in an unheated terminal while she was in transit to Raleigh. So on January 17, Mom picked up Lily from the breeders and drove her four hours to Toronto to catch a direct flight to Raleigh. An hour away from Southern Pines, it's the closest commercial airport.

The flight landed at 2:00, in the middle of the afternoon. Mike and I were at the barn earlier than usual so he could ride a few horses before we left for the airport at 1:00. I started bugging him at 12:30 that it was time to go. Still without a driver's licence, I had to rely on Mike to take me everywhere. We finally left the barn at five after one.

"We'll get there in plenty of time!" Mike assured me. It turned out that Mike was right; we needn't have hurried. When we got there shortly after 2:00, they still had to unload all the cargo. At 2:20, we heard Lily howling loudly and then saw her crate sitting on top of a pile of cargo that was being pulled into the terminal by a small tractor. The whole load, her crate included, was securely held in place by a net made of bungee cords. Since we had her importation papers, I expected to be able to take her home right away. However, we found out that we first had to get her papers approved at the veterinary station, a ten-minute drive away. Apparently, Lily cried loudly the whole time that we were away; the cargo workers were casting exasperated looks in her direction when we returned. Although they must have been used to having dogs in transit in the terminal, they'd just about had enough of her howling.

On the way home, we put the crate in the back seat of the car and rolled down the window to let in the crisp outside air. Because she could see us, Lily was quiet. At home, we put her crate in the kitchen/living room of Mike's small bungalow. I spent hours sitting in the kitchen with Lily on my lap.

When we drove to the barn every morning, Lily rode in the back seat of Mike's car. Once there, we put her crate in a small, quiet area where the horse blankets were stored. I let her out frequently and watched her carefully. She quickly learned that she was not allowed to go into the sand riding ring, so she sat patiently at the gate to the riding ring when I was there, alert to my every move. If I couldn't keep a close eye on her, I tied her to a tree in the sun where she could see everything that was going on.

Looking back, I'm sure that my parents were hoping that Lily would fulfil an important need. I'd always had horses, and although I loved dogs, I hadn't been at all envious of other riders who had them. Almost all of them did. While I'd always wanted my own dog, the extra work of having one while on the road just hadn't appealed. But I now had the time to look after a dog, and I was ready for the responsibility. As my horses had been when I was competing, Lily was completely reliant on me. I missed having an animal, so in my parents' minds, Lily was the perfect solution. Years later, I realised that they were absolutely right.

Gordon was the first horse that Mike rode each day. Tacked up and hooves polished, he'd be ready, tied loosely in his stall when Mike and I got to the barn at eight o'clock every morning. After Mike had worked

Gordon in the ring for about half an hour, he jumped off and I got on. Gordon and I then walked across the road and headed into the woods of the Foundation.

Once there, I could choose many different routes to follow as we made our way toward a huge field that was half an hour's walk away. I was conditioning Gordon, ensuring that he was physically fit so that Mike could compete him. I did his trot work, but Mike had asked that I leave what I considered to be the fun part, the cantering and the twice-weekly gallops, to him.

On a trot day in January, I was to do two sets of 15 minutes each. Between the trot sets, my instructions were to walk for five minutes. While Gord walked toward the field, I played film reels from the past in my mind—loose, disjointed scraps of my life with my horses. Since it had only been a year and a half since the fall that seemed to have changed everything, I still found it too painful to edit my recollections and weave them into a cohesive narrative that would be my memory of that time. Instead, I often revisited all the flashbacks that I had stored, playing endless rolls of unedited film tape in my mind.

At that time, the memories of my beloved past still sprung crisply forth. Not yet the slightest bit blurry, they were oh so sharp.

Now, I long for the clarity of those memories.

A unique pattern of leaking sap on the trunk of a towering, majestic old pine indicated where to turn. Gordon and I went right and made our way onto another broad, sandy avenue. We crossed the main trail, a wide expanse of loose sand that has been carved into deep ruts by the many carriages using the Foundation. When we reached the other side of the avenue, I guided Gordon to the shoulder, where he walked off the beaten path, next to the trees. Here, the fallen pine needles had knitted together to form a cushion that prevented him from sinking deeply into the heavy sand lying just underneath.

When I got to the 50-acre field, Gordon and I trotted for exactly 15 minutes. These days, my thoughts often slid from remembering the past to wondering about the future. How long would Mike be competing Gordon? Why were my parents and Mike not letting me start to compete again? Why couldn't I just get on with my life? I should be spending my time riding. After all, I was a rider, wasn't I? The fall was just a bump along the road of my life. Nothing had changed. Or had it? I was feeling more and more uneasy.

Finished the trot work, I headed back to the barn the same way I had come. It was getting warmer; the sun had softened winter's grip on the sandy soil. But the sun didn't assuage my apprehension over how life was turning out and my growing awareness that things were different. When would *I* compete Gordon again? I wasn't just somebody who exercised horses. I'd done very well in North America, and I'd competed internationally for my country.

Mourning

> We are different, we know it, and we would give much to have the dimensions of that loss understood, and thereby bridge the chasm between those of you who have not had this experience and those of us who have.[16]

As winter rolled into spring, I felt more and more miserable. In March, when the rhododendrons abundantly splashed colour on the South, my world was painted in dark, sombre tones. Even though I was living in the same environment as I had before I was injured, I was consumed by feelings of emptiness, longing and loss. I'd assumed things would return to normal, and they had, hadn't they? Then why was I so unhappy? At that point in my healing journey, I couldn't work it out.

My job was thankless. When I rode Gordon after Mike had finished training him in the ring, my responsibility was to ensure that he was in top shape, physically fit enough to compete at the highest level. However, I knew that there would never be any glory in it for me *until*—I wouldn't even contemplate *unless*—things returned to the way they had been. Most days I was in a funk because I was no longer the one who would reap the rewards. I still firmly believed that before too much more time had passed, my life would be exactly as it had been. Eventually, I'd be competing Gordon, wouldn't I?

Mike was training Gordon, so I knew that, for a while at least, it wouldn't be me who performed an accurate, correct dressage test. I could only vicariously experience the rush of adrenaline of the second day, the cross-country. Gordon was almost unmanageable in the start box, but I even missed those anxious moments. I longed for the heady feeling of jumping cleanly with time to spare, and with a horse ready to jump the next day. The satisfaction of jumping a clean round (not knocking down any rails) on the third day, and doing so within the time allowed, was a feeling that I remembered, cherished and missed terribly. But despite these restrictions, despite my growing unhappiness, I held on to my preinjury past. I clung to what I absolutely believed would happen. I would soon be the rider competing Gordon.

My driver's licence was reinstated in May of 1999, so my independence increased substantially. However, the added freedom left me feeling even more confined. I was healing, arduously climbing toward being self-sufficient and independent, but my steady improvement was making it difficult for me to live in the environment that had, for years, been my southern home. As I was getting better, I was becoming aware of painful changes that had been precipitated by the accident. Post-injury life didn't seem to be turning out the way that I wanted it to.

When spring became summer, my increasingly grumpy mood should have been a signal to me that there had to be a change. It was now almost two years since I'd been hurt; more than a year had elapsed since my first trip south. My healing had progressed to the point that I began to sense that my preinjury friends were treating me differently. I felt like I was no longer welcome in their world.

No longer was I included in the chatter about everyone's horses, nor was I part of the discussions about the competitions in which they were planning to compete. It soon became clear to me that they weren't really my friends anymore, that they no longer knew me. They didn't know how to cope with me now that I was healing. Looking back at those painful months, I can't blame my old friends. I had changed dramatically, while their lives had continued smoothly on. I could try to fit in, but to them, I would always be "head-injured." When I think of those days now, I give them the benefit of the doubt: I believe that they acted as they did unconsciously.

Before my accident, I'd been so engrossed with my equestrian life that it had never occurred to me that my friendships with other riders had been shallow; we'd had one topic of conversation, and our interests had been narrow. On a superficial level—"How are your horses? Where are you competing next?"—we'd been comfortable with each other before the accident, but we'd never had any discussions with any substance. We'd never asked each other how we truly felt about any issues other than those related to our horses. We'd been— and, at that time they still were — consumed by the equestrian world.

I gradually became aware of how not just my friends but the whole equestrian world viewed me. When I'd first flown down to Southern Pines in March of 1998, only six months after the accident, I'd come to watch Mike ride Gordon at the local horse trials. At that time, I was still a patient at Saint-Vincent hospital, blissfully unaware of much, including the shifted dynamics between me and the people from my old world. To be fair, I'm sure that most people living in my former world didn't know that six months is very early in the healing process after a significant head injury.

During the painful summer of 1999, it appeared to me that everyone from my old life was—I think unconsciously—pushing me back to March of 1998. People's expectations of me remained heavily influenced by how I'd come across at that early stage in my recovery. However, I had progressed far beyond that point and, as much as I tried to hide my head-injured self, it seemed impossible for me to do so while in the equestrian world. Thoughts of how my relationships with the others had changed—they now looked at me pityingly; they now considered me an outsider—resulted in unspeakable emotional pain. Tremendous, heartbreaking sadness overwhelmed me. It was a painful time.

My head-injured self, the one I was so desperate to leave behind, had become the only *me* that others in the equestrian world saw. They couldn't see past my injury; it completely overshadowed my equestrian self. Most unfortunately, I suspect that many were never able to adjust their vision as I continued to get better. I believe that they just couldn't relate to the evolving, growing, changing me as I rehabilitated.

Emotionally devastated, I realized that they weren't going to be there for me as I healed. My heartfelt wish was that everyone would find a reason to admire my climb out of the abyss created by my fall, but it seemed that it just wasn't going to happen.

My feelings about how others now viewed me were reinforced that June when, at one of the trials at which Mike was riding Gordon, I had spoken to the Canadian Eventing Team coach. I'd come away feeling pitied, frustrated and angry. Paul had looked at me through the same head-injury lens through which everyone seemed to view me. That brief conversation had left me asking myself a huge question: Would I ever be "Claire the equestrian" again? It forced me to acknowledge a harsh reality, one that I had refused to consider until that time.

As July and August grew hotter and more humid, the hours I spent at the barn started earlier and earlier each morning and stretched as far into the evening as the daylight allowed. I spent these endlessly long days feeling haunted by my past, smothered and suffocated by my surroundings. I couldn't imagine not being in Southern Pines, but at the same time, I was realizing that something had to change if I was to stay there much longer. It wasn't until fall colours had started to paint the few deciduous trees in the area that I at long last understood that there was only one way to assuage my unhappiness. For the first time, it occurred to me that I might be happy again if I left my old world. It had taken me two years since my fall to face the brutal fact that my familiar life was no longer.

That awful transitional time in my healing journey perpetuated another paradoxical development in my recovery. As I continued to get better, Mike and I were drifting apart. What he had seen in me as a rider—persistence, motivation, tenacity—had remained with me, and they were now helping me to transform into a person he didn't know at all. He grew tired of always being in the caregiver role, and I was tired of feeling as if my wings had been clipped. I no longer needed a caregiver. But even though I realized that it was time to move on, I was sure that losing him, after having already lost so much, was going to be too much.

Most importantly, I finally accepted that it would be disastrous if I were to reinjure my brain. My head and the brain inside it could not—ever—undergo that magnitude of trauma again. Only time had prevented me from acknowledging that harsh reality. The realization of that most painful fact only occurred when I had healed, cognitively and emotionally, to the point that I was able to recognize it.

After a serious head injury, some individuals are never able to see how they come across to others, how they belong or how they interact with others. It's a sad reality, but there are many who never regain the ability to step outside of themselves so that they can observe themselves and the way they are situated in the world. I became able to do so during the summer of 1999. This revealed to me that if I wanted to move forward, to keep healing, I would have to remove myself from my old world, to distance myself from the stigma and the label of "different" that the head injury had imposed. I had to escape the memories, the people and the places that could never, realistically, be a part of my future. It was an emotionally excruciating time, but I had to face facts.

I was ready for the head injury to be invisible. And, to make it invisible, I had no choice but to leave my old familiar life, to completely remove myself from the precious, cherished equestrian world. What made the decision even harder was that, although I would eventually discover that all people have a plurality of identities, at that time I was only aware of the equestrian me. So, what on earth would I do? I couldn't imagine another life. To my family and to Glennis, it must have seemed to take forever before my situation became so shatteringly clear to me. I was ripped apart at the core.

It would have been helpful to talk to a professional, but I was in the States, away from the rehabilitation available to me in Canada. Years later, I know that I should have been seeing a psychiatrist. A psychiatrist could have helped me realize much sooner that I couldn't resume my old life and helped me come to terms with the fact that, because of the accident, I had no choice but to reinvent myself and live a different life. But I'd had no professional to help me, so it had taken over a year before I figured out on my own that it was time for me to find new things to explore, new friends and new things to spark my interest. Everything had to change. I had to compose a new life so that I could escape from the ghost of head injury that was forever trailing me.

I knew I had to move back to Canada. Going home would enable me to get on with my life, to reinvent myself. I knew what I was going to do—what I had to do—so the fall months of 1999 were endless, agonizing and almost unbearable.

Back to Canada

Late October 1999

Burritts Rapids

On a cold, raw Saturday that was nudging November, Lily ensconced on the passenger seat of my Jeep, I drove back to Canada. As I was heading out of Syracuse, I got a speeding ticket. Somehow, my excuse that Lily was driving didn't work. All my belongings were stuffed into the Jeep. The only identity I knew: Claire the rider, the equestrian athlete—the one that I'd assumed I was since post-traumatic amnesia had left in January 1998—was quickly disintegrating. But I refused to let go of it completely.

Mike was still all-important to me. In late November of that painful year, he flew up to Canada. It took a session with Glennis, during which both of us talked, before it was driven home to me that Mike and I were done. Finished. The relationship was no more; the last tie with my old world had been cut. He must have felt relieved that I was no longer under his care, that he was no longer responsible for me.

Although I had unconsciously suspected what would unfold during the session with Glennis, I absolutely did not want to accept that the past I'd known had ended. Sadness, loss and heartbreak flooded my senses. Soon I was slipping down into a darkness similar to the one I had encountered in the spring of 1997.

What I needed to do was explore a completely different world. However, I hadn't yet healed to the point that I could realize the endless possibilities now available to me. When Glennis and my parents carefully suggested that I look at other avenues toward which to direct my energies, I didn't want to acknowledge that idea at all. I slid around in confused and depressing thoughts: I was a rider, wasn't I? Everyone around me understood that I was not yet ready to try something completely different, that I had not yet successfully severed the equestrian tie and released that fundamental part of my identity. I was bound and determined to keep riding.

For me, the new millennium did not signal a desire for change, rebirth or reinvention. Instead, mired in the aftermath of loss, I was desperate to hang onto the vestiges of my former self. Although I was grudgingly aware that some modifications due to my head injury were necessary, and although I had still convinced myself that riding was always going to be at the centre of my life, I did concede that my focus now had to be on another, less dangerous but still competitive, form of riding. My top-level event horses, Gordon and Sing, became show hunters.

My mother and I went to Pennsylvania in January 2000 to visit the stable of a trainer who would take me on. My horses were shipped up to Pennsylvania from North Carolina. It wasn't long before I realized that I was very unhappy. I was trying to make it work. After all, I'd always been able to before, so I thought—wrongly—that if I worked hard, things would return to normal. The trouble was that my normal had changed, and I still was not ready to acknowledge that hard reality.

As much as I craved the familiarity of the known, I soon found out that my life would never be the same. I went to the gym every day to run on a treadmill. I had always done that, so why shouldn't I do so now? I went to the barn daily, where I became increasingly frustrated with how I should now be riding. I had always been in control of the care of my horses, so it did not work for me to have them stabled in a professional's barn, under her care. Things that I had been on top of—among other things, Gordon's recurring eye infection—did not seem to be important to her. It soon became clear that the life into which I had tried to fit myself did not suit me, so only two months later, I went back up to Canada. Master Sing was sent to a retirement farm in Pennsylvania.

Always difficult to keep sound, he was now old enough, 18, that it was time to stop trying. I didn't want to bring him back to cold Canada, so I found a farm where he could live outside year-round with some other retirees. Gordon was shipped up to Canada so that I could ride him.

I was wholeheartedly supported by Glennis and my parents. They knew I didn't yet realize that my happiness was up to me, that I was the only one in charge of the direction of my life and my future, and that I had to figure out for myself who I was going to be. No one could or would do it for me.

The question remained, haunting me and crowding my mind: *What to do now?*

Now

It took years before I could dispassionately reflect on the first three years after I was injured. When I look back at what was one of the hardest times of my life, I think that the most painful part for me to realize and reconcile was that my great friend, Mike, had not considered that our relationship would continually evolve as I slowly and steadily recovered.

Mike had been shattered by my accident. For the first couple of years after the fall, neither of us could imagine that the narrowly focused life we'd been building, and the friendship that had been developing for years before we became involved, would never be the same. Mike had admired my tenacity as a rider. Although I was not nearly as talented as he was, I was as persistent, as dedicated. I don't think he'd come across someone like me in a long time. We'd been partners and soulmates; however, our relationship had been based solely on a life that revolved around horses. My injury, not initially recognized by either of us as life-changing, had stressed our relationship to the breaking point. Nothing would ever be the same.

Now, many years later, it's okay. We chat a couple of times a year. Mike recounts his days, solid and patterned. I relay what's happening to me. My days are full. I'm grasping at whiffs of inspiration, catching ideas and watching the changing weather outside my window as I write. I know he can't relate.

But I *can* relate to his stories. I used to be just like him.

I retreat to my wood stove; poking at its fire helps bring old moments to life. They're still there. Over the last few years, however, they've evolved into recollections of precious times, memories of a wonderful relationship that used to be.

QUEST

As the ill person gradually realizes a sense of purpose,
the idea that illness had been a journey emerges.[17]

Change

During the summer of 2000, I slowly came to terms with the cold, hard truth: the accident had forced me into a new reality. My new life would have to be one without horses in the forefront. Master Sing and Gordon Gibbons were still mine, but I had sold the other horses.

Riding had been part of me since I was a young child, but I'd never broken down *why* it was so important to me. I loved everything to do with my horses: their care, their training and competing them. I finally understood that, deep within me, my goal-oriented self had fuelled this passion, which in turn had ignited a single-minded pursuit of excellence.

I was still goal-oriented, and it took nearly three years for me to realize that this dominant facet of my personality was the same as it had been before the fall. But although I was still as driven and obsessed as ever, the accident was forcing me to find other directions in which to channel my energies, to discover new goals to work toward.

To continue healing, I'd have to find a new goal, one in which I'd find myself re-created and reborn. The endless time I'd spent in rehabilitation had left me feeling scattered and tired of being viewed as a survivor of a life-altering traumatic brain injury. That identity had been accentuated because I'd had to spend three years focused on my physical, cognitive and, most importantly, emotional healing.

I had no idea in which direction to now focus my energies, so for a few months I wandered aimlessly, without purpose. If I wanted to be happy again, it was fundamentally important that I find a new focus, a new path to follow that would be as fulfilling for me as my life with horses had been. I knew that the old me no longer existed, but who did I visualize being? What did I want to do?

I fervently hoped that my catastrophic fall and injury would not overshadow the rest of my life. I wondered how the injury and its aftermath could be seamlessly stitched into the quilt of me. The head injury still dominated all other facets of who I was. Although *survivor of head injury* would always be a part of me, I hoped that over time it would not be the sole identity that others saw. But I knew it would be who I was in the eyes of others until I found something to supersede it. It hadn't yet become only one part of who I was. I realized that it had to before I could move on.

What if I were to enroll at university? I'd always done well at school. If I tapped into my previously ignored academic strengths, my life could be completely different. People wouldn't even know about my history unless I chose to tell them.

I would never have admitted that returning to university was the easy way out, but if I did go to university, I wouldn't have to search for a goal. Working toward a degree would automatically provide me with one. I'd have a new identity—I'd be a student. In many ways, I think that university enabled me to redirect my single-mindedness. Instead of concentrating my energies on riding and horses, I immersed myself in head-injury research. It was only after I had graduated that I became aware of a more important reason for my return: going to university and completing a thesis would be important steps on my journey to find out who I was becoming.

The Next Chapter

September 2000
University of Ottawa

Thinking to myself that I must be crazy, I went back to university three years after the accident. I sure didn't feel like an academic. Truth be told, despite my father's wishes, I'd never felt like one. During my first foray at university, I hadn't been ready to view the experience other than as a way to acquire skills that I could use to make money to support my equestrian ambitions.

When I'd started working toward a BSc right after high school, I hadn't yet lived through the roller coaster of emotions that I had now banked. The accident had slowly peeled away the hardened outer shell that I had always worn as an elite athlete, one that had acted as an invisible coat of protective armour. I used to be impenetrable, tough, impervious to everyone and everything but my horses. However, that *me* was now gone, dissolved into the past.

When the journey began, my friends thought I was crazy to restart my education. "Don't you already have a BSc?" they asked. They were not even taking my history of the fall and its aftermath into account. Most of them simply thought that I was out of my mind.

"Why?"

"What are you proving, and to whom?"

"Are you not too old?"

I thought that I would apply to the Master of Arts (Counselling) program. As a counsellor, I imagined that I could be useful to retiring athletes as they transitioned to their new lives. I now wonder whether

I made this choice as just one more attempt to remain in touch with my former life. A condition of my acceptance into the program was the completion of three undergraduate psychology courses.

On a sunny September day, the first Thursday after Labour Day, I parked in the new parking garage on the corner of Mann and King Edward Avenue in Ottawa. Then, surrounded by other students, I trudged up King Edward's hill toward the campus of the University of Ottawa. My new knapsack slung over my shoulder, I was on my way to my first university class in over 15 years.

It's not a crazy idea, I silently reiterated until I reached the campus. While I walked, I repeatedly questioned what I was doing. What were my intentions? I couldn't believe that I was returning to university.

My first class was held in a huge lecture theatre in the psychology building. Projected onto the screen behind the lectern were the words Introduction to Psychology. There were over a hundred students sprinkled around the room. I assumed that most were first-year; they appeared to be only 18 years old. One girl was sitting by herself about halfway up the rows. Wearing a university jacket from another school, she looked to be closer to my age than all the other students. I sat down next to her and asked about her jacket. "University of Alberta," she informed me. She'd just moved here. "Rosanne," she said. We kept talking, and as the semester wore on, we found that we were distancing ourselves more and more from the younger first-year students around us. We were older, past the stage of staying up all night, drinking too much and surviving on unnutritious food.

In November, Rosanne asked whether I was interested in going to the ballet at the National Arts Centre. I was, so we started going to the ballet at the NAC together that fall of 2000. Sixteen years later, Rosanne is still a very good friend.

The course that Rosanne and I attended, as well as one of the other undergraduate courses I had to take, were incredibly difficult for me because they involved memorization more than any other type of learning. Although I function competently on most levels, it will always be hard for me to memorize material from a textbook rather than learning it through understanding. However, undergraduate courses often require regurgitation of memorized material. Although I tried my hardest, I could barely memorize well enough to pass the courses.

Every Monday, the professor in the class where I'd met Rosanne gave us a simple quiz on the previous week's reading and lectures. After I had written three or four of the quizzes, each of which I barely passed, I approached him and explained my trouble. He seemed to understand, and he told me, "I can't stand the idea of you spending the entire weekend trying to memorize a chapter on the structure and functions of the brain. I'll quiz you orally instead."

Initially we met right after the class to go over the chapter. He reworded each question for me several times, until he had almost given me the answer. After a couple of Mondays spent trying this method, it became apparent to him that this wasn't working either. My injured brain just had too much trouble coping with all the information in a chapter. He recognized this, along with the fact that I was trying my best.

"How would you feel if I give you a B for the course?" It was obvious to me that the professor didn't want to spend the time quizzing me orally. Of course, he did not know that it was the lowest mark I'd ever received. I now realize that his generous offer in no way fit into my understanding of excellence. In my mind, his concession to me only underlined my deficiencies.

I felt that the professor had relegated me to the must-pass-because-I-have-to pile. I wasn't in the excellent pile. I had grown up to interpret excellence in a particular way: if you're not the best, you try as hard as you can to be the best. As far as I was concerned, excellence was a way of being extraordinary, better than everyone else. But in this situation I felt pitied, as I had felt when I was in rehab. It seemed that my life was no longer in my control. When I'd been an athlete, I had always been in control. I'd tried to control everything, and I'd successfully controlled a lot: my own fitness; my horses' scheduling, training and fitness; when I rode them; what I ate; what they ate. But things were different now.

The second course was much the same as the first. However, the professor did not try to understand the difficulties I had memorizing the course material. When I scanned the mid-term exam results, I was devastated when I saw that I'd barely passed. In the end, I approached the department head and was given a pass for the course. Again, it was much less than I was used to.

I had a lot of fun in the third course, called the Psychology of Sport. We had to produce a diary of our lives during each week of the course. My creative juices flowed, and I composed a page for each week, jotting down my thoughts, adding little watercolours I had painted and inserting colourful ribbons as well as many other decorative items. Each student in the class also did an oral presentation. We were free to choose our own format, so I incorporated videos of my horses and poems I had written. I talked about the changes in my life. I got an A-plus for the course.

The concerted creative and unique efforts that I made in that class helped me to understand, comprehend and interpret course material. My efforts and individuality were being recognized and applauded. I learned that when I made sense of what I read and what I was taught, memorization was not necessary. Besides, comprehending material in this way would give me a more complete and in-depth knowledge of the subject.

Clinging with slipping fingers to my equestrian past, I rode Gordon a few times a week during that autumn of transition into an unfamiliar academic life. My old friend was stabled at a barn halfway between the university and my home. I rode after my classes, working him outside when it was not raining on those increasingly cold fall days. I loved every minute I spent riding in a big field all by myself. However, I often caught myself doing more harm than good, inflicting silent and indirect punishment on myself as I thought about how things had once been and compared them to how they were now. It bothered me that I was not looking after Gordon myself. Once again, I felt out of control.

Gordon and me, September 2000.
Credit: Betty Cooper, Sugarbush Studio

The Master's Journey

Winter 2001 to Spring 2004

After the three compulsory psychology classes, I had to complete five Master's of Education courses before I started the counselling program.

Full of trepidation, I walked into the classroom where the first of the Master's level courses, Child and Youth Development, would be held. I would attend every Wednesday evening for the next 12 weeks, from the second week in January to the middle of April. Fran Squire, the professor, came over and introduced herself to the students as they entered the classroom. Fran's bright, kind eyes twinkled from under her blonde bangs as she personally welcomed each of us, her handshake immediately quelling the butterflies in my stomach. I know now that she, too, was nervous; it was the first Master's level course she had taught. At the time, I noticed her hand was shaking. It wasn't long before she told the whole class that she was in the early stages of Parkinson's.

Immediately sensing a connection, Fran and I were soon telling each other the stories of our respective journeys. While the stories I shared were centred around head injury and the devastating accident that had changed my life, Fran's stories described her life before and after her shattering diagnosis of the progressive chronic illness Parkinson's.

When I went into the Graduate Cafe during the many years that I spent in the graduate program, Fran would often be there. She sometimes had to wait an hour or so until the start of the class she taught. The university had only a sparse room—no offices or lounge—available for sessional professors. Fran arrived at the campus early because, although

Parkinson's did not yet affect her in many ways, she found that it did alter her perceptions. She didn't drive, instead relying on buses to get her to the university. Fran became my mentor during my academic journey, frequently reading and then thoughtfully commenting on my class papers.

We attended and presented together at two conferences, sharing rooms at both. At a conference at Acadia University, we stayed at a bed and breakfast in Wolfeville, Nova Scotia. One evening, we rented the movie *Under the Tuscan Sun*. Lying in our respective beds as we watched it, we were only an hour into the movie when I heard sobs coming from the other bed: Fran was crying! She was very into the movie, very into the moment. After a while, I laughed at her. It would be a stretch to say that I laughed with her.

When I look back at this moment, I find it interesting to see how reserved I was. Fran had no trouble expressing her emotions by crying, but I kept mine under wraps. My still-sealed self, left over from my athletic past, did not permit such displays of emotion, instead it required absolute control. I was desperately hanging onto that time in my life, not yet ready to show my feelings even to a friend. Unbeknownst to me, I was still recovering. I've since discovered that my healing will never be complete.

Changes in who I was, and who I would become, were shoving their way into my conscious awareness while I was taking the compulsory courses before the counselling program. As the courses progressed, I was discovering that I wanted to engage in the reading, research and writing required of the Master of Arts curriculum. It would be much more work than the practical counselling program.

I switched into the MA program, which required the completion of a thesis. At the beginning of my adventure down its long and lonely path, I had plenty of time to wonder about the type of study I wanted to conduct. In each of the three required courses, I wrote a traditional term paper, and then I upped the ante by creating something that illustrated what I understood to be the theme of the course. One of the courses was called Creativity and the Arts. For it, I composed an artistic position paper, integrating information that I'd gleaned from class visits to the National Gallery of Canada, the Museum of Civilisation and the National Arts Centre. The rather creative interpretation I produced, artistic collages of our visits, was somewhat surprising to the professor—I'm not sure he knew what to do with it—but I'd been imaginatively inspired by these visits. He gave me an A+.

When I realized that the professors all admired my creative efforts, I started to feel a lot better about myself. I was standing out, my term "papers" were unique, and my marks reflected the extra effort involved in thinking about and then composing each project. I'm sure that none of the professors had any idea how much they were contributing to my personal growth at this critical time in my recovery. My self-esteem was bolstered, and I felt much more sensitive, more in tune with myself and with the world around me.

This very positive outcome confirmed for me that becoming a student had been the right thing for me to do. Before starting the program I'd hoped that the university journey would help me to become a very different person than I had been before—or, for that matter, since—my fall. At this early stage, I was already noticing how this new venture was changing me.

In the years before I was injured, I'd been math and computer-science oriented. Because of this background, I assumed that when I returned to university I would once again be looking at the world through a haze of numerical data. I was perfectly suited to conduct a number-crunching quantitative study, wasn't I?

However, that assumption had applied to my old life. Despite my background as a computer scientist, and although I will always recognize the importance of quantitative research, it soon became apparent to me that it didn't interest me to conduct such a study myself. Now I found myself to be nuanced, shaded, multicoloured, insightful and thoughtful. Rarely did I think left or right, yes or no. I no longer cared if my results stated conclusively that my proposed theory was right or wrong. Instead, I found myself drawn to others' stories. I wanted to interact with people, observe them during these interactions and then quietly reflect on what I'd learned while I was talking with them. The conversations with a study's participants, and my observations during those times, now meant more to me than the definitive results of a quantitative study.

When I first realized that my thinking process was changing, I was completely taken by surprise. It seemed that I was now more suited to qualitative research, which consists of an in-depth, descriptive exploration of the phenomenon under study. There are no right or wrong answers when a study is qualitative, and there are typically only a few people participating in the study. In a qualitative study, questions begin with why, how, what, when or where. There are an infinite number of responses to such open-ended questions.

Although there were countless opportunities for research, all begging for exploration, I found it relatively easy to decide on a study to conduct so that I could complete the requirements for a Master of Arts degree. Certain that I would be making a unique contribution by delving into the experiences of survivors of head injury, I contemplated how my own rehabilitation journey could be part of the study. I wondered whether I could somehow stand the life-changing traumatic brain injury on its head and use it productively to sink my teeth back into life. I realize now that I was likely subconsciously hoping that research into head injury would help me to incorporate the fall and its aftermath into my evolving self.

My curiosity was piqued when I read about autoethnography. After countless hours in the library, I had a greater understanding of it. The researcher is also a participant in an auto-ethnography. Researchers explore their personal experiences as well as those of other members of the same culture. By undertaking an autoethnographic study, I could reflexively delve into my own experiences as well as studying those of the other participants so that I could contribute to a wider cultural, political and social understanding of head injury.

Autoethnography is both process and product. Although I didn't realize it at the time, the process of autoethnographically studying head injury would be therapeutic. It would help me to work through the monumental changes to my life that the fall and the resulting head injury had imposed. The product would be twofold: for me, a step toward understanding what had happened to the evolving me, and for others, a fuller understanding of the culture of head injury.

After many years of turmoil and upheaval, I would once again have a goal.

However, at this relatively early stage of my emotional healing journey, I was not at all ready to strengthen my association with the culture of head injury. I didn't want to be identified as "one of them," so I wondered whether my choice of research topic would situate me very visibly and squarely within the culture. I felt a bit trapped by head injury and worried what implications such a study might have on who I was and who I would become. As my journey of rehabilitation, growth and recovery moved forward, I wasn't at all sure that I wanted "survivor of head injury" to become a prominent part of my identity. Although it would always be a part of me, I didn't want to acknowledge it, much less accept its presence. However, my choice of research topic made it difficult not to acknowledge that being a survivor of head injury would always be a part of me.

Gotcha!

Captured.

You can't get away.

Forget it.

It only took a split second,

but that impact

changed my life

forever.

I can't get away.

Emotional pain and

heart-wrenching loss

were shoved
down my throat.
I still can't get away.
So I researched,
and now write about
Traumatic Brain Injury.
I will never get away.

As my ideas for an MA study began to take form in my mind, I grew more and more excited. I arranged a meeting with Glennis, the one who had been my therapist after the head injury, and her business partner, Pierre.

"Hello, hello. How's it going? Let's sit in here." Pierre led us to small meeting room that was set up like a living room. It had cozy chairs conducive to talking. Once the three of us had settled into the chairs around a small table, I began to enthusiastically run my ideas by them.

"You're aware that I created an artistic interpretation to accompany the term paper I wrote for each class? Well, I felt so good after completing each creative project that I would like to examine how other survivors of head injury feel after the same experience. I want to explore the impact of creative activities on the self-esteem of individuals after head injury. How can creative activities be used for cognitive therapy and rehabilitation? Why does creative involvement bolster clients' self-esteem? From my personal experience, I know all too well that after a head injury people often feel marginalized, pitied and looked down upon."

Pierre and Glennis listened to the ideas pouring out of my mouth, and they looked at each other in amazement.

"Amazing serendipity!" said Pierre. "We've just opened a workshop where our clients can work on creative projects! At Creative Hands, clients—with or without the help of a therapist—design, plan and then construct something artistic, either useful or not. Their art may be created with the help of a scroll saw, several of which have been installed at the facility. Very safe to use, scroll saws enable the clientele either to work on their own designs or to work from a pattern."

Pierre didn't stop there. He informed me that clients could go to Creative Hands any time; there was a social club-like atmosphere, one that encouraged casual conversation. The convivial environment of the facility took the emphasis off the history of head injury that's common to all the clients. They could relax and talk informally about other things. Although there was always a supervisor present, watching carefully but unobtrusively, none of the professional barriers that exist in the clients' relationships with therapists at the parent clinic were noticeable at Creative Hands. Engaging in creative activities encouraged survivors to unconsciously explore alternate ways to understand their new, post-head-injury worlds. There was also an added, unseen benefit to being a client at the facility. It was a site for informal learning opportunities. A creative project involves planning, designing, implementation and, importantly, completion. The therapists had noticed a marked increase in self-efficacy, which is a person's belief in his or her own ability to complete tasks and reach goals.

Pierre and Glennis graciously allowed me to use Creative Hands as the site for my Master's study. I collected data over a six-week period, during which time I spent two or three hours a week with each participant, all four of whom Pierre and Glennis had suggested. Near the end of the data collection, one of them, Jim, insightfully summarized the impact of the study on its participants: "When you've had a brain injury and survived ... I believe that you can learn a great deal about the 'new' you after you've completed a creative task."

When the data-collection period was finished, I approached Rob, the occupational therapist at site of the study.

"Rob, I want to get everyone together for a focus group interview." So we set up a meeting for the participants. While we sat together and chatted informally about the study, I watched and listened as they enthusiastically asked each other about their experiences while completing their creative projects. The session was a fruitful addition to the other forms of data I had collected.

The focus group had provided fascinating and very revealing conversations, from which I composed a play. Creatively interpreting the data in this form inspired me so much that I decided to relay my personal story, which would also become part of the thesis, as a metaphorically written tale. The tale symbolized my journey of healing until I returned to university in 2000. Then I represented the study's results pictorially, painting them onto a four-by-six piece of plywood. Four long pieces of seaweed represented the four themes I had discovered. There were five fish—I was one—representing the participants, swimming in between the strands of seaweed.

I had fun composing the thesis. I really enjoyed creating and crafting, shuffling the thesis's chapters around, trying them in different places. The job was complicated because parts of the thesis's mix were alternative representations in the form of focus groups, stories and art. What order would make the most sense? Finally, when I assembled the whole thing, it was a composition of narrative, art and creative nonfiction. The thesis, "Creatively Rehabilitating Self-Esteem After an Acquired Brain Injury: An Auto-Ethnography of Healing," creatively rehabilitated my own self-esteem.

The path toward the Master's was not at all like the academic program I'd completed as an undergraduate years ago. At that time, I'd derived a sense of accomplishment from the prize—a degree. I'd approached my studies toward a Bachelor's degree in computing science purely as a way to financially profit from a university education. This time around, however, the journey itself had fulfilled me, not just the fact that I'd successfully completed the program. The experience had been very different than I'd expected. I was surprised at how much I'd enjoyed the past few years, and I was also surprised when I was nostalgic at the journey's end. In the spring of 2004, I received my degree, a Master of Arts in Education.

Although it had been hard work, the Master's degree had provided me with a goal. I suspected that what I'd personally experienced while working on the degree was also what was happening to the participants of my study. When I saw the light at the end of the tunnel during the study's final stages, I became sure that I would be able to complete the MA. My self-efficacy, or my belief in my ability to complete a task, increased immeasurably. This, in turn, had a very positive influence on my self-esteem, my confidence in my worth and ability. Attaining the degree, accomplishing what I'd set out to do, was a huge leap toward the re-establishment of my self-esteem. Similarly, completing a creative task had increased the self-esteem of each participant in the study.

The MA degree left me feeling incredibly self-assured, signifying to me that I'd taken control of my life again after my world had been forcibly changed almost seven years ago. The resulting head injury could have left me with severe deficits, no longer cognitively able to be the sole author of my own life story. Instead, I could resume composing my life.

Although I was now focusing on academia, I steadfastly refused to completely give up my equestrian identity. But that year, a huge part of my being was ripped from me. Reluctant to let go of my equestrian life entirely, and comforted by the familiarity of my trusted friend, I had ridden Gordon a few times a week during my first years in the Master's program. But in the spring of 2004, it became apparent that my buddy needed to retire. His body had been used up by the international level of competition we had taken part in. In June, I sent my beloved friend to Pennsylvania so he could live in the milder climate as Master Sing had. There, he grazed in a field, enjoying the sun and the peacefulness of his old age. But later in the summer, his tired feet could hold him no longer. When I got the call, I sobbed, broken-hearted. But there were no options. Gordon was put down on August 28, 2004.

Gordon is the last horse I rode. I haven't ridden in over 12 years, and I find that I have no desire to ride. Someday I'll explore why. Even though it's been a long time, I don't feel emotionally ready to open that jar of feelings. The question is, will I ever be?

The PhD Years

2004–2005

My family was completely surprised when, to keep all avenues of possibility open, I applied to the PhD program during the last year of my Master's work. My father was thrilled. He had encouraged my return to school, but I think that a PhD was beyond even his wildest dreams. Although it would have been preferable to change schools, I wanted to go to the same university at which I'd done my Master's. I didn't want to be uprooted. My friends were there, my life was there.

The PhD degree promised to be a new goal toward which I could channel my energy and enthusiasm. I was still very competitive and driven, so taking action toward it, as opposed to just thinking about the PhD program, made sense to me.

Even though everyone told me that the PhD was incomparable in every way to the MA, I was game to give it a go. The MA journey had been long and somewhat stressful, but I was—at least initially—blissfully unaware of how strenuous the PhD journey would be. Putting my nose to the grindstone, I read an endless quantity of dry scholarly books and academic journals. I wrote papers—more papers than I'd previously thought would ever be possible for one person to produce.

2006

Early in 2006, it was time to choose the topic for my study, and I knew exactly what I wanted to explore. It would be another qualitative study of head injury, and it would be another auto-ethnography. As well as being the one conducting the study, I would also be a participant. I wanted to look at other Olympians and professional athletes who had sustained head injuries and listen to their stories of healing. What did their stories, and their body language while they were telling their stories, reveal about their journeys of identity construction after their head injuries?

In July, I was getting ready for the PhD comprehensive exam when James Wright called me from where he was vacationing in Cape Cod, Massachusetts. I'm still close to James, my first riding coach who is in the real estate business. A couple of years earlier I'd asked him to keep me in mind if he heard of a house that might suit me. I wanted to be on the Rideau River, as I already was, but closer to Ottawa. I'd been living in a lovely contemporary house on the river, and it had spoiled me in terms of what I expected of a property of my own.

James, who never moves quickly but always with much thought and consideration, was phoning to tell me about a house that I needed to move on right away. An old stone house on the river, it was not closer to the city but a five-minute longer drive. I knew the house. Behind a low stone wall, a gorgeous stone house called *Gilnockie* nestled along the banks of the Rideau River.

James's assistant showed me the property the next day, a Friday. The house was small, with one big bedroom and two smaller ones. Old houses do not have ensuite bathrooms. In this one there was a small bathroom on the second floor, with a three-by-five-foot bathtub/ shower. There was a powder room on the main floor. The house had no mudroom; one walked from outdoors straight into the kitchen. There was no washer and dryer. Since the ice storm of 1998, the owners had only used the house on the weekends.

My parents had told me many times that in 1963, when they bought the stone house in which they still live, they would drive by *Gilnockie* and hope that their house, which at that point was barely more than four stone walls in the middle of a hayfield, would eventually look as nice. Of course, now their farm is lovely. It is beautifully taken care of and surrounded by the abundant greenery of lawns, trees and gardens of my mother's flowers.

But was this stone house suitable for me? Because I was in the middle of my PhD studies, I absolutely had to have high-speed Internet access, and there was none here. Also, there was no room that could be used as an office. Walking out the back door, I found myself on a lawn stretching out behind the house. When I reached its edge, I saw a steep bank of about 50 feet dropping down to the water. Yes, the house was on the river, but the river seemed to be inaccessible.

Next I explored a narrow bit of lawn leading away from the kitchen door; it was lined with huge piles of rotting, unusable, firewood. After 200 feet, this avenue opened. I couldn't believe my eyes. I was in a clearing of a couple of acres. There was an old metal barrel that had been used to burn trash sitting in the middle of the space, and an enormous pile of dead branches seemingly waiting to be burned lay near the steep riverbank. There were also half a dozen centuries-old oaks and maples, spaced on the grass as if on the parkland surrounding an old estate in England. I was enchanted—and very excited!

"Mom, Mom! You have no idea what I've found." My mother had come along to see the house, her burning curiosity easily winning out over her other commitments. She followed me back into the magical space I'd discovered.

"Wow, this is unbelievable! What a surprise—you really don't expect it to be here." Trees, thick along the edges of the property, hid the space from the road. Exploring further, we found a path that led out of the meadow and away from the house along the edge of the riverbank. First on level ground, it then wandered downward. At its end, we came upon an old boathouse, seemingly unusable, sinking into the river.

It was perfect. I was captivated by what I soon learned was called "the meadow" by the owners. There seemed to be many places where I could put my own stamp on the house, as well as on its lovely property. There were lots of details that needed to be worked out quickly; we only had the weekend. The owners would take bids on the property in the real estate office that Sunday at 6 p.m. It was already Friday morning. I jumped into action and arranged a home inspection for Saturday.

A strategic detour on Sunday morning had me driving past the house. I'd intended to pull over outside the gate to look, think and imagine, but I found myself behind a car being driven by an older woman, with a man sitting in the passenger seat. It turned into the driveway. Could it be the owners? I took a chance and followed them.

"Hi, Dr. and Mrs. Armstrong? I'm Claire Smith. I think you've met my parents; they live only five minutes away."

"Oh yes, of course. Nice to finally meet you." I didn't say anything about looking at their house. I just wanted them to recognize me later that day when I made an offer. We chatted briefly, and then I drove home.

Introducing myself to the owners may have been instrumental. That evening, when James's assistant and I went to the agent's office to make an offer, the owners recognized me. I didn't have to wait long before the agent came into the room where we were waiting and told me that the house was mine.

The stone house I'd just purchased was built around 1832 by the engineers of Colonel By for a Mr. Jenkins, who'd received a grant of land from the Crown when he decided to remain in Canada after the completion of the Rideau Canal. The previous owners had named the house *Gilnockie* after a 16th-century tower house located near the Armstrong ancestral home in the Hollows, Scotland. They were delighted that I wanted to retain the name.

When I explored the options for high-speed Internet, I discovered to my horror that because of the tall, ancient trees on the property, I couldn't establish a clear line of sight to any of the local service providers' towers. I was left with no option but to erect a 200-foot tower that points directly at the main tower in Merrickville. Thank goodness it's not very visible from its location next to the log "garage." I didn't yet have an office on the property, but at least I had Internet access. I made frequent use of it during the evenings, with my computer cradled on my lap in the living room.

Although both the house and its grounds are magical, when I first bought the house, the lack of a mudroom presented a problem. Just one person's winter jackets soon overflowed the hooks to the left of the door into the kitchen. And because there was no room that could be used as an office, I "commuted" the five minutes to my old office. No one had yet rented the lovely modern house that I'd vacated, so I staked claim to its office until a tenant was found.

That fall, just when I was finally emotionally regrouping and settling into the new *me*, my right foot started to drag. I didn't have time to worry about my unusual gait; after all, I was midway through the PhD program. There were plenty of other—more important, I thought at the time—things to think about. For the first few months, all that was wrong was that my right foot touched the ground as I brought it forward. My right ankle didn't bend much, so the toes of my right foot pointed down and dragged midstride. Once, when I was showing a friend my new property, my right foot caught on the grass. Down I went, ending up sprawled on the lawn. I brushed off the problem as insignificant.

Early 2007

It was just a few more months before walking became something that I could no longer take for granted. Most people don't have to think about walking, but I could not mindlessly walk. I had to make a conscious effort with each step I took, thinking about over-bending my knee so my foot would clear the ground. In April, I was—quite literally—dragging my foot as I trudged along the PhD path when I noticed in the University of Ottawa newspaper an announcement of a new book by Cheryll Duquette of the Faculty of Education. Years ago, a Cheryll Duquette had been my teacher.

In 1974 I had been one of 10 students in the grade 8 "gifted" class at Kars Public School. On the first day of school, we had all crowded around the windows of a portable classroom on the grounds. Curiously awaiting the arrival of our new teacher, each of us hoped to be the first to see her. A Triumph sports car, its roof opened to the sun, sped into the parking lot, and a tanned young woman climbed out. Was it her? Hurrying away from the window, we were sitting innocently at our desks when the door opened.

"Hi. I'm your new teacher, Cheryll Duquette. It's the first year of this enriched program, and it's my first year of teaching." When I'd walked by her before recess, I'd been impressed by how tall she was.

I thought the author of the book just might be the same Cheryll Duquette—it was not a common name—so when I was next on campus, I knocked on the door of her office. The door was pulled open by a woman who was much shorter than I am.

"Hi, Cheryll, I'm Claire Smith. My curiosity got the best of me."

"Claire! I can't believe it! Wow, it's been over 30 years since I saw you last! I was in my first year of teaching!"

"Yes, a long time ago. I remember you being tall."

"And you were at least a foot shorter than you are now. You were just a kid. I was concerned about you. You were so young, and there's so much more to school than just the classes." I'd been eleven in Grade 8, a couple of years younger than the others because of my acceleration through the lower grades.

I reassured Cheryll. "Thank goodness I made a great group of friends in high school. Since that time, my life has evolved so much." She invited me to sit. I only stayed for a minute though, sure that she had lots to do.

"I'm so glad we've reconnected. Are you interested in any RA work?"

I told her I was interested in doing research assistant work; then we hugged and I was off. The next year, she offered me a position. I did a literature review as part of the preparation for a study in which she was involved.

In June, less than a year after I'd purchased *Gilnockie*, I decided that I should build an office there. I was also desperately in need of a mudroom. Choosing an architect whose ideas appealed took several consultations. The one who won the job imagined an airy office space joined to the kitchen by a narrow mudroom. When the architect was designing the addition, I insisted that while in the kitchen, I had to be able to look through the mudroom and down the Washington Mall, the name with which I'd christened the avenue leading from the house to the meadow. The mudroom, only six feet wide and with a full glass door, still pleases me daily. The architect planned the adjoining office to be a soaring space with huge windows and three skylights. Because a full bathroom, including a washer and a dryer, were also in the plans, I would no longer have to "commute" to do my laundry.

On August 28, 2007, my artist friend, Joyce Devlin, turned 75. She held a party at her home in Burritts Rapids, to which she invited many of her old and new friends. Food, wine and art welcomed me when I walked through the door into the festive house, a portent of how special the evening would turn out to be. Only a few minutes after I arrived, I noticed Michael Rowland coming in the door.

"Hi, Michael. I'm Claire Smith. We've met a few times over the years." More than 20 years had passed since I'd driven out to his studio, so it was hardly surprising that Michael looked older. The fit, long-haired hippie of over 20 years ago now had short, neatly cut white hair. A slight paunch revealed that many years had passed since I'd seen him last. I figured that he must be in his mid-fifties.

I was sure that Michael didn't remember the first time we'd met, so I told him the story:

> More than two decades ago, I was home in Canada for the summer. For my birthday in April, I'd been given a new Michael Rowland handbag, one of your elegant, purse-like backpacks. You create the most beautiful leather handbags! I love that they're one of a kind, each one custom crafted from cowhides. But, although perfect in every other way, my birthday backpack was just not quite big enough. When I finally got around

to taking it back to your store in Merrickville, it was almost four months later: August 1, 1995.

"Why don't you drive out to his workshop? It's at his house, only five minutes away," the saleslady at the store helpfully suggested. So on that cloudless midsummer afternoon, I headed out toward your home and workshop, two miles along a country road out of Merrickville.

After turning off the road, I drove up a long driveway that led through a thick stand of evergreens, and I pulled up at the workshop behind your house. Laughter greeted me: three bare-bottomed children were running through the sunshine, darting back and forth under a sprinkler's mist and the rainbow it created. The verdant produce in an enormous vegetable garden bordering the driveway glistened from the spray. You were standing just outside what appeared to be the entrance to your workshop. Mid-forties? Untrimmed beard, long grey curls caught in a ponytail.

I introduced myself. "Hi Michael, I'm Claire. I was sent here by your sales assistant. I'm hoping you can help me." I know that these days you no longer do custom work, but at that time it was no problem to ask you to tweak a design in some way. In your workshop, I fingered layers of gorgeous leather hides in sophisticated, elegant colours. They were draped over rows of sawhorses, and their subtle odour wafted gently over me.

"This one. Can you make me a backpack like the one I have?" I pointed to a soft brown hide. "Only slightly larger, out of this leather?"

After measuring for the changes I wanted, you promised me that it would be at the store in two weeks. Back in the car, I drove away from hippy paradise.

I'll always remember that day. Not because of the leather backpack I craved. And, I hate to admit it, not because of you, the man who makes them. The date will forever be easy for me to retrieve because, although I was expecting to listen to a stimulating interview on CBC radio on my short drive home, the program was instead suddenly interrupted for a special broadcast. The news was startling, bleak: Brian Smith, a well-liked sportscaster in Ottawa area who had been shot the night before, had died.

When I finished, Michael said "Wow. What a terrible reminder of the day you came out to the farm. When I lived out there, I was still married. And you're lucky that I made those changes, because I don't do custom work anymore. I'm now living in the apartment over the store in Kemptville. You know, in that big old stone building. I bought it a few years ago."

"You've fixed it up beautifully. What a gem of a building! It needed someone to love it. I bought an old stone house on the other side of the river a couple of years ago. I'll show you around sometime if you like."

"That would be great! Can I pour you a drink?" Michael asked. "You look like a white-wine person."

We were soon joined by others, and we chatted with many of the friends that Joyce had gathered together from her eclectic life. Everyone marveled at the paintings Joyce had hung; they were just a few from her enormous collection.

"Dinner's on!" Joyce announced. The enormous pot of homemade vegetarian chili that had been bubbling softly on her stove was ready to eat.

The evening sparkled with friends, food, wine, warmth and cheer. When it wrapped up, Michael walked guests to their cars. Everyone had parked in the pitch black of a rural road. I couldn't believe how dark it was. Thank goodness for Michael's flashlight.

"Expect a call. Come for dinner and a house tour," I said to Michael.

"Thanks, Claire. I'd love to."

A few days later, when I was in Kemptville, I stopped at Michael's store.

"Hi, I'm glad you came in." He probably thought he'd sell me a purse, but I was there to invite him over for dinner.

"How about that house tour? Can you make it over after work today and stay for dinner?"

Soon after I got home at 5 pm, I had shrimps on the grill and basil pesto in the making. I boiled pasta until it was al dente. The warm shrimps wilted the uncooked spinach that I had spread in a flat, wide blue-and-green porcelain bowl. When the shrimps were cool, I stirred in the pesto and the pasta. Michael arrived at 7. We lingered over dinner and wine, our conversation begging more.

The light was fading when I showed Michael the property. "This trail winds down to the old boathouse. One of these years soon, I'll build a new one. Spectacular location, isn't it?" Supported by an old cedar whose trunk I was clenching with my left hand, I leaned toward the river. "Here, have a look."

Michael took my place on the tree and exclaimed, "Wow, unbelievable! Completely private, and what a view."

The next night we met in a lovely restaurant, the one after that I had a book club meeting. Michael came for dinner once more the following week, and he didn't go home. We established a pattern. Before long, he'd moved in.

It was becoming more and more difficult for me to walk. As time went by, the mysterious stiffness slowly travelled up my right leg. By Christmas 2007, my leg wasn't bending much at the knee. I started to swing my leg out to the side when I was walking so that I'd clear the ground. But there was so much going on in my life that, although I was extremely worried about my gait, I shut it out of my mind. I tried to push it aside, but it was getting harder to ignore the puzzling problem. What on earth was going on?

Something's Wrong

2008

In January 2008, I submitted an abstract to a conference held yearly by the International Brain Injury Association. This prestigious conference is always very hard to get into, so I didn't hold out much hope. Six weeks after I sent off my proposal on the closing date, an email from the conference organizers arrived. Giggly, I called Michael at work.

"Guess what! I've been accepted to present at the conference in Portugal! I'm going to fly over the pond to Lisbon, all for eight minutes in the limelight! I hope you'll come!" It would look great on my CV—was that the excuse I needed to go all the way to Portugal? Michael had never been overseas, so the adventure became twofold: his introduction to Europe and my presentation at a top-tier conference.

In June, Michael and I flew from Ottawa to Lisbon. I had reserved a room at one of the conference hotels, which turned out to be a lovely one in a busy location near the centre of town. Michael found it fascinating to study the workings of everyday Lisbon. He spent hours leaning against the window of our room, enthralled by the parking system outside the hotel. Peering through his binoculars, he figured out that people were giving a man who lurked in the area all day some change and their car keys. The man then shuffled the cars every couple of hours, so their drivers avoided getting parking tickets.

Intrigued by the traffic detour around the square below our window, Michael noted the lineups, honking and yelling. Fascinated by the locals, he studied the park within the square. Bent-over, shuffling women with kerchiefs tied underneath their chins sprinkled birdseed, while innumerable pigeons crowded them and impatiently pecked the ground around their feet.

Very usefully for me, my resourceful partner also discovered that the hotel was on a direct tramline to the conference site. While I attended the first day of the conference, Mr. New-to-travelling-outside-North-America was more than happy to spend it exploring Lisbon on his own.

While I was at the conference that first day, I ran into Shawn, a rehabilitation doctor based in Ottawa whom I'd met previously. He was appalled when he saw me walk.

"Hi, Claire. How long have you been dragging your right foot? Is anyone looking into the problem? Make an appointment when you get home. I'd like to see you as soon as possible." Shawn sounded concerned.

Almost two years had passed since I'd started dragging my foot. I certainly hadn't shut my mind to the puzzling symptoms—I was extremely worried about what was happening to me. But because I was so focused on my studies, it may have appeared to others that I was not overly bothered by my worsening gait. I'd been to see a neurologist, but I was resisting agreeing to a long investigation into what was going on. If I didn't admit that there was something wrong, the problem would go away, wouldn't it? I didn't want anything encroaching during the very focused time of my PhD studies.

"My family doctor referred me to a neurologist; he hasn't yet figured out what's going on," I told him. "A couple of days after I get back to Canada, I'm flying out to Calgary, where I'll be collecting data. Remember Dave Irwin? He was one of the Crazy Canuck downhill skiers. He also skied at two Olympics."

"When you're back, then. I don't like what I'm seeing."

Although I was thrilled to be presenting, I knew that most of the conference wouldn't interest me. The session detailed the results of number-crunching quantitative studies. My presentation was scheduled on the second day, in an auditorium with at least 300 seats. An overflowing success, the room was packed. It was standing room only;

people lined the walls. I like to think that the conference attendees were thrilled to attend a qualitative presentation. I could just read their minds: *What the hell? Art as rehabilitation?* They all seemed to be listening carefully; there were questions and comments. When I'd finished my presentation, the room thinned out significantly before the next presenter started. I stayed for her presentation, and the next, out of courtesy. After that I was gone, finished with the conference, ready to experience Lisbon and its surroundings with Michael.

Seeing the old European city through Michael's eyes was delightful. We took a tram that stopped several times while it climbed up one of the city's seven hills, cautious before venturing forward around the blind corners of the steep, narrow streets of the old city. The facades of centuries-old buildings nestled up against "sidewalks" that were just narrow concrete strips crowded between each building's old stone exterior and the street. Yet more kerchiefed women tossed yet more birdseed. Cars were parked along the streets, wheels up on the sidewalk, squished close together and angled sharply to fit into the smallest of spaces.

Everywhere I went, my right foot dragged, leaving an unusual track behind me. Despite my outward attempts to ignore the issue, I was deeply bothered that Shawn had been so concerned about my puzzling gait. But although I'd seen doctors, I was avoiding looking the problem straight in the face. Refusing to stray from my academic path, I convinced myself that I had no time to deal with whatever was wrong, that it would go away if I refused to acknowledge it. The only thing that was important was finishing the data collection for my PhD.

I'm fine.
Can't you see?
I'm collecting data
for my PhD
and working through the final stages
of grieving for who I used to be.
There is nothing wrong with me.

Soon after I got back to Ontario, I flew out to Alberta, where I stayed for four days with Dave Irwin and his partner, Lynne. Every morning I walked, with some difficulty, down the main street of Canmore to the coffee shop where Dave met with other men for a couple of hours. It was late July when I headed out West again to collect data from another participant, in Victoria, BC.

In both cases, I gratefully accepted invitations to stay with them as their guest while observing their lives.

Dystonia

During the summer I'd had a couple of appointments with the neurologist, but he hadn't yet come up with an answer. As the summer became fall, I stayed as busy as I could. By doing so, I thought that I wouldn't have time to think about my deteriorating gait. I may have denied worrying, but nothing could stop me from worrying silently inside. My attempts to allay my fears by ignoring the issue didn't work. I knew something was very wrong.

I was still running, but I found myself buying new running shoes much more often than I had in the past, because the toe of the right shoe would wear out in no time. One sunny day in September, I tripped badly. Scraped raw by the gravel onto which I'd fallen, my knees and elbows bled profusely. I walked home. The incident scared me so much that I stopped running.

What on earth is going on?

That September, there were still two participants from whom I had to collect data, when after a long process of elimination, the neurologist finally diagnosed the chronic illness Dystonia. It had taken a full two years since the puzzling symptoms had first appeared for the doctors to rule out other possibilities.

Originating in the brain, Dystonia affects the muscle movement of the affected limbs. It can affect one muscle, a muscle group or the entire body. Striking about 1 percent of the population, this chronic illness strikes more women than men. In my case, Dystonia was probably triggered by my head injury, which had left a couple of lesions on my corpus callosum, the fibrous area connecting the two hemispheres of the brain. This bundle of nerve tissue contains over 200 million axons, which transfer motor, sensory and cognitive information between the brain hemispheres. My doctors suspect that in my case these lesions are located in the area of the corpus callosum that is used to transfer the motor information governing the muscles of my right leg. My brain tells my right leg to be ramrod straight if there is any weight on the bottom of my right foot.

Right leg to brain:
What are you saying?
Why are you bellowing
"STRAIGHTEN!"
as soon as my foot is in contact with the ground?
Every time my body's weight is shifted my way,
you yell at me, insisting,
"LOCK YOUR KNEE IMMEDIATELY!"
You hiss,
"YOUR LEG MUST BE RIGID!"

When the neurologist told me that he believed I had Dystonia, I shattered inside. His pronouncement instantly erased the feelings of increased self-esteem, self-confidence and self-worth that had been gradually building up since my return to academia. It wasn't lost on me that the timing of his diagnosis was impeccably set to interrupt my emotional recovery from the devastating head injury. The diagnosis of Dystonia decimated my still-fragile psychological state. I descended into a darkness like the one I'd experienced when I'd first realised that my equestrian identity no longer existed.

The only way that I could muster the emotional strength to finish the PhD was to shut my mind to Dystonia's presence and its insidious progression. I avoided thinking about anything other than my doctoral work. Like an academic ostrich, I buried my head in the PhD sand. Because I couldn't see Dystonia, it didn't exist.

However, although I was trying my hardest to ignore Dystonia's presence, it wouldn't let me escape. The chronic disease that had subtly revealed itself when I started to drag my right foot in 2006 had continued to worsen, the symptoms inexorably creeping up my leg over the next couple of years. By the time the neurologist made his diagnosis, my right knee would lock completely whenever I put any weight on my foot, so I would swing my right leg out wide while walking to avoid tripping. I was tired even when I walked only short distances, 100 feet or less. Soon I was walking as little as possible.

Adrift: off course, disoriented, confused. Unsettled, aimless.
I am adrift without "normal" movement.

As dark as those days seemed, I later realized that there were certain things I should be thankful for. At the time, I was sure that there was no angel in sight, but I will forever be grateful to the angel that I now know was watching over me. It wasn't until I was in the last class of the PhD program, nine years after the head injury, that Dystonia first reared its ugly head. By the time it was diagnosed, I had almost finished collecting data.

I wonder now about the other possible outcomes. If Dystonia had wormed its way into my life a few years before it did, when I was in the middle of completing my MA degree, would I have been able to muster the strength to carry on and plough through the physical and emotional swamp that lay ahead? Would I have commenced the PhD program? Would I have wanted to? If I'd started the program, how would I have collected the study data that involved close, in-depth observation for five days?

What was Michael's role throughout the intertwined PhD and Dystonia travails? By nature, Michael is a caregiver. Lavishing love and attention comes naturally to him. We had become a couple just before the perplexing right-toe dragging made itself evident. I lapped up the attention, and the dinners—Michael is an excellent cook. Consumed by both the PhD and Dystonia, I didn't even think about how he fit into my life. I just needed to be loved and cared for at that precarious stage of my life, so I felt lucky to have him.

It wasn't until I'd completed the PhD journey that I was able to consider his role in my "new" life. Did I want or need a caregiver? Would I feel stifled?

When I finally finished my data collection near the end of 2008— after spending time in October with 1960 Rome Olympic canoer John Beedell, and former professional hockey player Jim Kyte in November—I had no choice but to finally address my deteriorating walk. Although Dystonia had been diagnosed in September 2008, only in November did I finally call Shawn, the doctor who had shown concern in June in Portugal. Over the next year and a half, he did every possible test to confirm the diagnosis, and then he tried to mitigate the impact of the illness on my life.

Despite his efforts, my right leg will forever try to straighten when I'm standing on it.

Drugs,

gait analysis,

Botox,

acupuncture,

more drugs;

I can't walk much—

at all.

No way.

Not a chance in hell.

Are you kidding me?

. . .

I guess not. Nothing's working.

Almost there

2009–2010

I spent 2009 at my desk, surrounded by reams of data, which I first transcribed and then analyzed. It was the early months of 2010 before I had composed the first draft of my thesis. In the spring, I met with my committee on a couple of occasions. Each meeting led to more revisions. Reworking the thesis until they were satisfied, I finally submitted it in July.

August 2010
Edmonton, Alberta

My uncle, a medical doctor in Ottawa, had become interested in acupuncture a few years before I was diagnosed with Dystonia. On several occasions he'd travelled to Edmonton to train in the ancient Chinese technique with world-renowned acupuncturist Dr. Aung. Grasping at straws to find something—anything—that would keep Dystonia from advancing further, I flew to Edmonton in August 2010 for a two-week treatment session with Dr. Aung.

While there, I stayed with a good friend from the Master's program at the University of Ottawa. Terrie Lynn had moved out to Edmonton to do her PhD at the University of Alberta. Her husband, Ian, was (and still is) head chef at a country club there. I went to my acupuncture appointment every morning and spent fun evenings with them. The three of us often caught a play; it was the time of the local theatre festival.

The time in Edmonton was academically productive. Most afternoons I worked on an article I planned to submit to a journal, carefully composing a paper chronicling my data-collection experiences with one participant, whose name was Linda. I'd spent a very interesting time with her while collecting the data, even though eventually I had to cut her story from my far-too-long thesis. When I got home, I submitted the paper to a refereed journal, and after several rounds of resubmissions, it was finally accepted. I am the sole author. Although I had published several papers for which I had drawn material from my Master's thesis, this was the first that would be published about my PhD work. I will always be haunted by the phrase "Publish or perish," which had been drummed into me by the academic community.

I was in Edmonton for two weeks. The whole time, I waited anxiously to hear when my thesis defence would be scheduled, impatiently checking my email several times a day. But the email never did arrive while I was there. I had 10 sessions with the acupuncturist, but they didn't help at all. Dr. Aung and I were both disappointed. We hugged when I left, and he wished me well.

September 2010
Merrickville, Ontario

In September, a couple of days after I got home from my disappointing trip to Edmonton, the email I'd been waiting for finally arrived. The message informed me that I would be defending my thesis at 10:30 a.m. on November 18, 2010. Despite the quickly approaching momentous event, Dystonia tried to reign supreme. On the advice of Dr. Aung, I made an appointment to see my uncle, the medical doctor trained in acupuncture, right after I returned home. The fact that David is my uncle was not a problem, because according to traditional Chinese medicine, it's ethical for him to treat me. I had acupuncture treatments twice a week for the next month, but it was to no avail.

The neurologist that I'd been seeing, the one who had finally diagnosed Dystonia, had prescribed two medications, but they hadn't in any way mitigated its relentless progress. He prescribed a third one, but so far it wasn't helping. The chronic illness continued its inexorable advance. However, I was still refusing to acknowledge the cruel reality of my situation, and I was ever more adamant that I didn't need a wheelchair.

November 2010
Merrickville, Ontario

It was only a week before my thesis defence. When I think back and remember that anxious, stress-filled final week, I'm appalled that I was oblivious to the fact that my dog could hardly make it up the three steps out of my office. How could I not have realised that Lily was having trouble walking, that her hind end was giving out frequently? I couldn't have counted on Michael to notice. I'm all too aware that he always avoids any difficulty with his family, me, his friends and, it then became clear, our dog.

Michael, that wonderful man, shies away from anything hurtful, anything requiring assertive action on his part. It's the way he is. I've learned that wakes, funerals and any other emotional decisions, our dog's well-being being one, are up to me.

One morning during the second week of November, my head was filled with academic thoughts. For the last couple of months, I'd been blind to most of what was going on around me, but my eyes finally opened when I saw Lily on the front lawn, struggling to stay upright. She was swaying and falling over. Reality crashed down onto me. I hadn't been there for my dog, who'd been there for me. Her hind end was failing.

From the time that she'd arrived in Southern Pines in 1999 at only eight weeks old, she'd always been as close to me as was possible, my loyal companion. She lived through the "same-as-always days" when I'd been determined to continue my old life with the horses, going with me to competitions up and down the East coast. She had unconsciously supported me through my upheaval from that life, through a speeding ticket, a Master's degree and now to the brink of a PhD degree.

The earliest available appointment at the vet clinic was 11 a.m. Although it was just eight in the morning, I called Mom, who quickly drove the five minutes to my house. She was no doubt worried about the dog, but she was more concerned about me. A hugely important and very significant event in my life, my thesis defence, was only a few days away. At that moment, however, my faithful dog was all that I could think about. When Mom came in the door, Lily, who had been lying beside my desk, struggled to her feet. Lily wobbled up the three steps leading from my office into the mudroom to greet my mother. I watched in horror—she could hardly make it up the steps.

Ashamed, I realized that I'd had blinkers on. I had been reading, thinking and preparing for my defence. When I look back, I'm heartbroken that I didn't notice the obvious. Lily had not been eating well for a few weeks, and I'd been tempting her with delicious treats of chicken and leftover steak. But I was preoccupied. If I'd been more aware, I would have worried. Golden retrievers are known for devouring everything in sight. Now, I'd do anything to turn back time so that I could give Lily the attention she needed, and deserved, after those many years she'd spent by my side.

When Mom, Lily, and I arrived at the vet clinic, the receptionist had to help us persuade Lily to enter the building. It doesn't matter how unwell dogs are, something about a vet clinic causes them to plant their feet and refuse to walk in. When it was our turn, the vet felt Lily's tummy, and then she turned to us. I didn't even have to listen to her; I knew exactly what she was saying. But I wouldn't leave Lily there, at a cold clinic she hated. It had to happen at home. We arranged for the vet to come to my place at 3 p.m.

The clock inexorably ticked on. My mind heard it loudly, from the time that we got back home around noon until that most dreaded moment. Lily lay in my office, right behind my desk chair. I constantly fed her dog cookies, the only thing she would eat. My Dad came. Michael, realizing the awfulness of the moment, arrived home. Finally, the vet crunched down the gravel driveway.

I wasn't ready yet. But would I ever have been?

"Okay, let's go." Dad carried Lily up the stairs and out the mudroom door. I couldn't stop the tears. Dogs always seem to know. Lily lay down on her side on the grass outside the door. I held her tightly for the vet; soon she became completely still. Her body lay there for a couple of hours, until the nice man with a backhoe who lived just down the road arrived to dig a hole under a sculpture at the end of the grass, which I call the Washington Monument. Then he respectfully carried her body up the Mall and laid her to rest forever.

The loss of Lily made it close to impossible to put my emotions aside and concentrate on my PhD defence. I don't know whether my thesis committee could have related to the loss of a dog. Did they have dogs themselves? If not, did they have a clue about how meaningful dogs can be to their owners? They had, of course, no way of knowing what a key role Lily had played in my recovery from head injury, so I would have been surprised if they'd understood why Lily's loss had affected me as much as it had.

The sadness over my loss of Lily accentuated the dark cloud that had been hanging over me for the last three or four years. Although I was still not ready to acknowledge the fact that there really was something wrong with me, I *had* been diagnosed with a chronic illness. My mysterious symptoms, which had first appeared in the fall of 2006, had led to a devastating diagnosis. However, so intent was I on avoiding my disability that I couldn't even consider facing the reality of my situation—I needed to use a wheelchair most of the time. Although I had never wanted anything less, I grudgingly purchased a portable wheelchair so that I could sit and be pushed if I had to travel any distance. That distance was rapidly becoming shorter and shorter.

Despite the endlessly painful distractions of those difficult days, I didn't want to waste time thinking about anything but my defence. Even though my dog had just been put down and I couldn't walk worth a damn, I still had to defend my PhD thesis in less than a week.

The PhD Defence

November 18, 2010

The University of Ottawa

There are several locations around the campus that are used for thesis defences; luckily, I was very happy with the one chosen for mine. It was accessible, and importantly, it was smaller, a more intimate room than others that are sometimes used. As is the case for all PhD defences, my thesis committee, made up of three professors from the university and an external examiner from England, all sent me questions for my consideration a week or so before the date.

I had no trouble with most of the questions, but they did require a fair bit of reading and time. After I had researched my responses to these potential questions, I turned my thesis around and around, upside down and inside out, thinking of all the different angles from which I might be interrogated. I read and I read. I thought about the committee members' areas of interest outside of my thesis. Could they possibly have me talk about the thesis in a way that appealed to those areas?

I would be given somewhere between 10 and 15 minutes by the chair of the defence, a professor from another faculty, to outline my study. I would have to squeeze a lot of information into a very short period. My Powerpoint presentation began with an explanation of why I had chosen to do this study. After reviewing the purpose of the research and the questions I had explored, I planned to glide briefly over the review of the literature, describe the methods I had used to gather the data, explain how I had analyzed the data and then—at last—talk about what I had found. I would finish with the study's contributions. I had also prepared several more slides to hold in reserve in case I needed to refer to them if I were asked certain questions.

On November 18, my father, who seemed to be more nervous than I was, drove me into the city. In no time we were on the Queensway, the major east-west artery in Ottawa. The traffic was light, but Cruddums' hands were clenching the wheel.

"Just talk. Forget about your notes. Look at the committee. PowerPoint is overrated."

I was thinking that my PowerPoint presentation would help me *not* look at my notes.

Cruddums parked and then unloaded my hated portable wheelchair—the distance we had to cover was too far for me to walk. I was resigned to the ritual that followed.

"Damn, just sit there while I find my glasses." I waited patiently in my chair.

"Wait till I get my brothel creepers on." I wasn't even wearing boots; the little snow that covered the ground was hard-packed, but Cruddums was reaching for the rubbers he slipped over his shoes to protect them from snow. Leaning into the car, he fumbled around; it took a while before he found his glasses and the brothel creepers.

"You wearing a scarf? It's nippy out."

No, I'm not wearing a scarf. It's less than 100 feet to where we need to be.

"We'll be inside in less than a minute, so let's just get going." I was about ready to scream. Cruddums locked the car and then wheeled me the short distance to the hall, remnants of snow crackling under the wheels of the wheelchair.

We'd arrived almost an hour early, my over-punctuality a lasting remnant from my athletic days. I had plenty of time to set up everything. One of my friends on the PhD journey was there and showed me how to use the PowerPoint console.

Everyone—except for my father—shuffled into the room where the defence would be held. My mother and Michael, who had come together in another car, were also excluded. To their collective dismay, I banished them all to the hallway outside. The only ones I allowed into the room were Glennis, my head-injury counsellor, and Fran, the professor who had taught my first Master's course and was now a dear friend.

My PhD colleagues and a few friends, as well as some PhD candidates who were a year or two behind me, were all there to support me. After they had filed into the room, I waited calmly while the people who run the university's thesis defences tried unsuccessfully to phone up the external examiner in England so that he could join us in a teleconference. They soon found out that they had the wrong number. They then emailed him. Finally, after almost an hour's delay, we were underway.

Because of my previous life in high-level sport, I could minimize my nervousness on this momentous day; the delay didn't faze me as much as it could have. When I was an athlete, I'd visualized every one of my performances many times. These visualizations had incorporated all sorts of possible variations, as well as the many potential problems that could crop up. Fortunately, these mental tools were still available to me.

I'd pictured my PhD thesis defence in the same way as I'd visualized those many competitions in years past. Still, I'll admit that this day was extremely significant and not only in terms of my journey of recovery. A successful defence, even if my injury was discounted, would immediately change who I was—and who I was becoming.

Finally, the defence began. The chairman introduced the committee and welcomed the external examiner. He then announced that I had 15 minutes to talk. I was pleased; I'd been expecting only 10 minutes. The longer time would make my job of summarizing the work so much easier.

But what usually happened next didn't happen this time. Usually everyone, including the candidate, is asked to leave the room. While the candidate and the audience are gone, the thesis committee strategizes and decides in what order the questions will be asked. However, the chairman didn't follow this expected procedure. Instead, he invited me to begin the overview of my thesis. Not only was I surprised, but judging from the faces of the committee members, they were as well. Although the routine he followed was unconventional and I was taken aback, my visualizations of the defence served me well. Taking a deep breath, I started to talk.

I took the full 15 minutes allowed to present my work. Then the questioning started. The first to go was the examiner in England. As is the custom, I'd emailed my PowerPoint to him the day before and had designed some extra slides to address issues he had raised in his feedback after reading the thesis. When he began, I breathed an enormous sigh of relief; it appeared that he had looked at the slides and had noticed that I had spoken to his concerns. He sounded very casual and non-confrontational, so I quickly felt at ease. My thesis advisor asked me afterwards if I'd heard his dog barking in the background, but I'd been so focused at the time that I hadn't noticed.

The questions from the other committee members were next. I'd anticipated most of them and had prepared notes. When everyone on the committee had had a chance to ask questions, they all had another turn. I was still calm and felt little anxiety over any of the questions. A couple of hours passed.

When the committee was finally finished, I wheeled my way to the hallway outside, followed by the rest of the audience. The committee remained in the room to decide my fate. Michael and my parents were standing in the hall, anxious and full of questions. But I just sat there— silent, drained and exhausted.

It seemed we had been waiting nervously outside the room for hours, but it was only minutes before the chair opened the door.

"Congratulations, *Doctor* Smith!" There were hugs all around. My father presented me with a beautiful plant. When I emerged from my postdefence fog, I realized that it was a lily. It seemed that, in spirit, my dog had been there for me all along. Because the whole process had been delayed an hour, everyone soon had to leave. It was about three in the afternoon, late enough that, when the few people remaining headed to the university café to cheer me on as I drank from the "mug of knowledge", the café was closed. We found a restaurant downtown that was still open for lunch, so my family, Michael and I were joined by Fran and Glennis for a much-needed meal and a glass of wine. My thesis advisor didn't come; she had scheduled a meeting with another student. Despite her absence, we were bent on celebrating. No "mug of knowledge" for me, but as I look back, the fact that I'd not sipped from it was not important. Instead, the missed drink was a portent of my future in academia.

What Next?

Early December 2010
Merrickville, Ontario

The journey that had occupied all my time for almost six years—ten years if you include the MA—was at long last over. I was wondering what to do about a thesis dedication. It isn't necessary to include one, and I didn't want to single out one person from the many who had been my supporters. It suddenly came to me: my dog, Lily, had been a huge part of the journey. My desertion of her during the last weeks of her life will always haunt me, so the dedication is both an apology and a heartfelt thank-you for her years of faithfulness during what was a most difficult time of my life.

For Lily
Thank you forever
for your constant and loyal companionship.

Whenever I think about the dedication, I smile to myself. It's not at all obvious that Lily is a dog.

After my successful defence, my parents gave me a horizontal gravestone that read Lily, 1998–2010. The earth was too frozen to install it properly, so in the spring we sunk the flat stone. It now lies level with the lawn at the base of the Washington Monument where Lily is buried. During the summers of the years following her death I often stopped my golf cart to see the tombstone, to remember my faithful dog and to clip the grass encroaching on her stone. When I realized how appropriate the site of her grave was, I wrote a nonfiction story about it. The groundhog and the log cabin are real, and everything in the story did happen.

When I took possession of the old stone house where I now live and the six acres around it, the first thing I did was to install an invisible fence to surround the three acres closest to the house. When I moved in, Lily checked out the whole area, including the lovely log cabin that had been moved into the backyard a long time ago. It sits nestled among several trees as if it has always been there. The unassembled logs must have seemed like the pieces of a puzzle during its reconstruction. I can still make out the Roman numerals carved into each log, which helped with the cabin's reassembly in its current location. Tiny and with no electricity, the cabin does not leak, and there is full standing headroom in the middle. It is now a repository for lawn furniture in the winter, but I dream that one day I will move a desk in and carve out a territory to write. I can look through the window and gaze out over the river below. It's peaceful, quiet.

A groundhog was resident under the cabin when I moved to the property. I first saw its hole when I bought the house. I could always see where the hole was but for a long time I didn't catch sight of the groundhog itself. If he ever appeared, he must have had a clear view of my office, a striking addition to the stone house, from the other side of the back lawn. I can see the cabin and the entrance to the hole beneath it from my desk. For the first couple of years, I thought the hole was old and abandoned. I wanted to fill it with rocks and earth because I was worried that it was undermining the cabin above, but I had not yet done so. I think Lily was happy that I hadn't. Her golden retriever genes kicked in at the thought of a groundhog. She would lie beside the hole, never tiring of the endless pursuit of imagined prey. Maybe she did tire; I saw her on a hot July day several summers ago, stretched out on her side next to the hole, seemingly fast asleep as she soaked up the sun. Was she really asleep? If I had been the groundhog, would I have dared tiptoe past the enemy? I guess not; as far as I knew, at that time he never peeked his head out of the hole. I assumed he had moved long ago, leaving the large gaping hole as a reminder of where he had once lived.

However, it appeared that the groundhog did still inhabit the hole. As time went on, he got braver. I saw him a few times—I assumed it was a *he* because he was enormous, so I am making a somewhat sexist assumption, but maybe *he* was a large female— venturing out and waddling across the lawn behind the house. The groundhog appeared to be not as fearful of Lily as he should have been. I imagined what his life was like, mainly sleeping and foraging for food. I must have caused trauma to the groundhog when I planted daffodil bulbs around his hole. A couple of years passed, and Lily stayed on guard.

The groundhog grew more and more complacent, and I would see him occasionally during the summer months. He dared to dart, as fast as his considerable size would allow, across the back border of the lawn when the dog was home. One blisteringly hot August day a few years ago, I was on the terrace, drinking lemonade with a friend while sitting in the shade of an umbrella. We suddenly heard a dreadful noise, a high-pitched call of panic. I ran as fast as I could toward the commotion. I raced from the terrace into my office and tore through the office into the mudroom. Out the door I flew and hurtled down the broad stretch of grass known as the Mall toward the abstract sculpture that I call the Washington Monument. In the little group of trees just behind the Monument, I could barely make out Lily, who was facing the groundhog as he stood on his hind legs, screaming in complete terror. Then I saw the dog grab the groundhog and shake him quickly. I covered my ears, but the end was so quick that there was only silence. I made my way back to my friend, who was still sitting in peace on the terrace. Lily followed in a couple of minutes and lay down by my side. A true retriever, she had cleanly and quickly killed the prey by breaking his neck and then left him for her owner.

When Michael came home, I told him what had happened. We pulled the enormous dead groundhog out of the trees and put him in the wheelbarrow to take him to his grave. He is buried a few metres beyond the invisible fence. I think that Lily was probably a bit lost after she'd killed the groundhog. She seemed to know the hunt was over, the groundhog gone forever. In the last years of her life, she no longer sat outside the hole.

Lily is gone now. She was put down a little over a year ago at age 12, her body riddled with cancer. She was a most faithful friend and my trusted companion through the forced retirement of my beloved sporting identity. She then accompanied me during the pursuit of my next goal, the long, arduous and seemingly never-ending trek toward my PhD. Lily died just before I had completed my academic journey, so I was not able to share my proudest accomplishment with her. I buried her under the "Washington Monument," and she is immortalized by a gravestone engraved Lily, 1998–2010, which is placed at the base. I wanted her to lie there because I love looking out the mudroom door, down the Mall, to the abstract art at the end. I thought it was a beautiful final resting place. It later occurred to

me that she would be pleased as well because the clump
of trees behind her grave is the site of the groundhog's
demise, her own proudest accomplishment.

In the days after the defence, a sense of completion and of accomplishment
wafted over me like incense. I had "toed the line" and played by the
rules as I'd ventured along the PhD journey. The PhD degree meant
that I had regained the status that I had become accustomed to during
my years as an elite athlete. Affixing PhD to my name came with
implications. Someone who has been awarded a PhD is a well-regarded
individual who has gained inclusion in a distinguished community of
readers and writers. PhD recipients have demonstrated their abilities to
pursue their own thinking, with added sophistication.

The degree would give me unique opportunities. By completing
it, I had demonstrated that I possessed the knowledge and skills to
learnedly explore my culture, with the hope of educating others about
head injury as well as helping those living with the consequences of such
a life-changing, traumatic event. More broadly, I hoped to enlighten
everyone I could about the challenges faced by individuals experiencing
a wide range of disabilities extending beyond head injury.

I just met the deadline. By submitting the final copy of my thesis
30 days after the defence, I was able to attend convocation in June
2011. First, I made the changes required by the committee, and then I
obsessively edited the thesis. Next, I returned my outstanding library
books and, lastly, I delivered three copies of the thesis to be printed
and bound. Finally, after pressing on during this final sprint, I could
breathe normally again.

The seemingly endless slog had finally come to an end. Suddenly, my
baby—my thesis—was finished. Done. Gone. For the first time in
years, I had no deadline to meet. Dead tired, I was disappointed to
feel the way I did after all I'd accomplished. I'd reached the heights
of academia, only to feel exhausted. I asked myself whether achieving
a MA and a PhD had been worth it. On dark days, it was hard to

convince myself that the degrees, as well as the journeys toward them, had been valuable steps in my recovery.

I expected to be thrilled because I was finished—but instead I felt loss. Rather than being exhilarated after achieving a PhD, I found myself experiencing the opposite. At the time, it seemed to me that my state of mind was unusual. I'd assumed such a successful ending would be a happy, positive event. The academic journey had ended, but instead of serving as a springboard to a new way of life in a presumed normal form—as an academic, author or lecturer—it had become a source of depression and loss for me.

Eventually, I learned that I was experiencing a typical reaction of loss after completing a PhD. I'd thought that I was familiar with loss; after all, a huge career-ending crash had changed my life completely. Rather than feeling restricted by the injury resulting from the crash, I'd used the accident to inform my research. When I'd refused to accept any of the physical and psychological challenges I faced as limiting, I had astounded everyone by instead plumbing their depths.

Did that explain, though, why I was experiencing the achievement of my PhD as a loss? I felt as though I'd been set loose—there was no longer a goal to strive toward as there had been the whole time I'd been working toward my PhD. I was having trouble coping. I had climbed to the peak of academia. When I thought about my previous accomplishments and how diligently I had pursued them, I wondered whether the actual PhD degree was what was important to me. Or, was it perhaps the fact that, while on the PhD journey, I had once again put myself in a position from which I could strive for excellence by pursuing a goal? Previously, that pursuit had been athletic; had it then become academic? Rather than the actual degrees, had the quest toward a goal been the reason for attaining them?

Pursuing and defending my degrees successfully had taught me to question, to wonder and to probe. Academically, I'd long known that I wasn't only a student, that I didn't have just one identity. No one did. It was becoming clear to me, however, that I'd only ever acknowledged two identities. Until I was 34 years old, I'd been a rider. For all those years, it had never occurred to me that I had other identities. When I could no longer be a rider, I'd become a student and had clung to that identity for 10 years—even though intellectually I knew better.

Over and over, I silently asked myself the same question: If I have so many identities, what are they? This was an old, familiar question that had occasionally risen to the surface since I'd been able to live my life fully following the head injury. I'd assumed that my journey of education would have given me the skills and tools to explore this nagging question. But had it?

Now that I had a PhD degree, the question wouldn't leave me alone. After my successful thesis defence, it became irritating, insistently pestering me for answers. Although the question gnawed at me as I searched for ways to make it stop bugging me, I rationally knew that a finite answer would never be possible. I finally realized that I sought not just an answer but also thoughtful insights into why I felt hounded. Why did the question that asked me who I was, and who I was becoming, bother me so much? I needed to stop it from haunting me.

Until Christmas, all I did was recline in various positions on the sofa in front of my wood stove. My main activities during that period were stoking the fire and reading. I bought almost everyone on my Christmas list a novel online, the shopping style best suited to my limited mobility. During my postdefence funk, I carefully removed the dust jackets from the books, replacing them when I was finished reading; the books still looked brand new. I slept for hours.

A large part of my problem was that I had not yet emotionally processed the head injury, even though the accident had occurred many years earlier. Before I'd returned to university in the fall of 2000, I hadn't yet reached the stage in my healing journey where I could constructively address the lingering emotions of loss and enormous change that were part of its psychosocial aftermath.

During my academic years, I never felt ready to *really* face the emotional repercussions of my injury, so I'd stamped it down. *Be quiet!* To be able to complete the PhD, I'd shoved aside some of the most complicated emotions, emotions associated with the event that had changed my life forever. I still believe that it was the right thing for me to do at the time, so that I could focus on my studies. While I was working on my PhD, facing these complex emotions would have uncovered many layers of unresolved feelings that might have resulted in emotional pain—pain that might have complicated and compromised the in-depth conversations that I was having with the participants. They had all gone through healing journeys after TBI and no doubt had their own issues, past and present. My conversations with them were fundamental to the data collection, so it was important for me, while talking with the athletes in the study, not to be wrapped up in my own life and its worries.

It was now high time to confront the few raw, painful feelings that were still lurking within me. I had to deal with the unresolved emotions left over from my TBI. I couldn't put off facing them any longer. For years they had scratched insistently at the surface of my psychological health. My churning mind could picture the raw feelings banding together, wanting to break down the door behind which I kept my unresolved emotions and insisting that I process them.

I wanted to be emotionally healthy again.

However, I was still refusing to come face to face with and admit to the real reason for my depression. When February came and my sombre mood didn't improve, it became clear that I hadn't touched the demon that refused to budge from its seat at the centre of my emotional well-being. I'd been completely avoiding the confrontation. After a while, I realized that it was incumbent on me to finally admit to, and address, the real source of my slump: Dystonia. No one else was going to do it.

In the months preceding my defence, I had travelled to see doctors in the United States. The physiatrist, rehabilitation doctor Dr. Marshall, had done a gait analysis, injected my right foot with Botox and fitted me for a brace. I had tried acupuncture. Nothing had improved my deteriorating gait. It hadn't help my state of mind to find out that treatment only works for a small percentage of Dystonia cases.

January 2011 marked a looming appointment with my neurologist at the Ottawa Hospital. I was very worried because I had noticed a huge deterioration in my gait. The neurologist had prescribed a series of drugs over the course of the previous couple of years, but nothing had worked. The last drug he had prescribed did not seem to be alleviating the symptoms of Dystonia in the least.

"Dr. … meet Dr. Smith." My mother, who had accompanied me because she was worried about my psychological state, proudly announced my new status to the neurologist I'd been seeing.

"Great! Congratulations."

Silent, I didn't graciously accept his congratulations: *I'm sure he thinks that qualitative research is not* real *research.*

"Let's go into the hall, and I'll watch you walk."

I supported myself on the wall as I walked awkwardly away, and then I turned and wove back toward the doctor with my other hand supporting me.

"Okay, come back into my office and sit down. So that medication hasn't helped? Thanks for coming in." The doctor shook my hand and left the examining room.

"When does he want to see me again?" I asked my mother. She rushed out after the doctor, and she didn't look at me when she returned.

"I don't believe it, but he says he doesn't want to see you again."

I stared at her as my world came crashing down.

Back in the car, my mother ranted: "That's insane!" Her hands gripped the wheel. Slumped in the passenger seat, my world swirled, and then it splintered into a million pieces.

Years later, I'm feeling somewhat generous. *Now* emotionally healthier, I think that the neurologist likely meant that there were no other drugs that he felt were worth trying. Because he couldn't help me, there was no point in seeing him again. But at the time, I was psychologically fragile, so I understood his dismissal differently. In my mind, I was a hopeless case as far as he was concerned, not worth spending any more time on.

Shattered

March 2011

Gilnockie

It was soon March, January and February having been ripped from my emotional calendar. The disinterest shown by the neurologist had certainly not helped my shaky psychological state. However, the harsh reality was that I no longer had any choice but to finally face Dystonia. It had become a pervasive presence, shaping my life in many ways that overshadowed everything else, including how I thought of myself and how I believed that others perceived me.

Although I'd always been tough and resilient, it took being dropped by the neurologist to make me realize that I could no longer shrink from the chronic illness that was staring me in the face. It had crept up on me during my PhD journey. I'd probably made the right decision to not let it interfere with my pursuit of the degree. Now that I'd completed the PhD, it was time to confront Dystonia.

Finding medical support for Dystonia was apparently up to me. The neurologist had tried to treat this perplexing illness with several medications and they hadn't worked, so why should he see me again? I would have to be my own advocate, both physically and emotionally.

I felt that I had done a lot of coping. I had climbed out of the virtual abyss created by my head injury, returned to university and then, despite everyone's expectations—although I'm very sure that none were quite as high as mine—graduated with a PhD. But when I thought about it, was what I had accomplished since my injury a surprise to those who know me well? Probably not, because as my PhD research suggests:

The path of recovery from serious injury is suggested by the path of life before the injury occurred.

I had never just accepted things that had happened to me, especially when I'd been unhappy or uncomfortable with them. I'd always needed to think, question and ponder when dealing with the unexpected, the unplanned and the unforeseen. So when Dystonia paraded into my life during my PhD journey, I didn't stand up straight, salute it and accept what it was doing to me. Not at all. Luckily for me, when Dystonia struck, instead of rolling over and playing dead, the guard dog who sleeps at the gate of my life had risen to its feet and bared its teeth. Barking and growling, it had not *accepted* Dystonia. I conceptualize the notion of *accepting* Dystonia's intrusion as resigning myself to its presence, instead of researching its causes, symptoms and treatments. I will never just accept Dystonia. It was never "meant to be" part of my future.

No one, of course, could have foreseen that chronic illness would become part of my life. As Dystonia insidiously progressed, I gradually became less and less able to walk. It soon became clear to me what I was up against, and I seriously wondered whether I could cope with this added complication to my life.

Dystonia's relentless progression resulted in depression—despair, misery and anguish. I found myself facing a seemingly impenetrable wall, insurmountable from where I was situated during those dark days. I had faced such a wall in the early spring of 1997, but I'd managed to surmount it and perform well with my horses until I had fallen at the European Championships that September. In December 1999, when I left Southern Pines for good, another "down" had swirled around me, challenging me to find a way out. That was when I'd finally had to acknowledge the harsh reality that a life focused on horses was no longer viable.

It's extremely difficult, if not impossible, to undergo any negative life change without feeling loss, sadness and grief. Before psychological healing can be contemplated after a huge life event, individuals must figure out what's causing any negative emotions that they are experiencing. It's not often obvious, so that step can be hugely difficult. When I was living in Southern Pines, beginning a year or so after I was hurt, it took months before I slowly came to understand why I felt lost and lonely. These were months during which I gradually realized that I would never be who I had been, that I would always be a person who had sustained a head injury in the eyes of those living in my former world.

It wasn't until I was back in Canada that I'd let myself experience my head-injury losses and the resulting anguish. At long last I'd had the courage to delve into the hurt I'd been avoiding. I'd finally let myself wallow in the emotions and feel them. I was raw. Bleeding. Aching for the old me.

In the early years of my involvement with horses and riding, I'd had no choice but to learn how to cope with and withstand the tremendous highs and lows inherent to the sport. My resiliency, my ability to cope in adverse situations, had been essential during my equestrian life. Then it came into play again when I called on it to help me crawl out of the morass I found myself in when I finally acknowledged that I could no longer be a rider. Now I hoped that my resiliency would come to my rescue once more. It was high time I faced the devastating changes and hardships caused by Dystonia.

Although it may seem evident to some that one would feel despondent after two major losses, it wasn't obvious to me. Instead, I was taken aback and very disappointed in my lack of ability to cope with my wavering emotions. I'd recovered psychologically from the head injury, but once again I found myself far from emotionally healthy. Even though I may have appeared successful to anyone watching, it didn't take me long to sink down as Dystonia tried to claw its way into who I was. As it did, I fought its presence. I had a wheelchair, but I convinced myself that I didn't need to use it to get around my house. Nope. Not me.

April 10, 2011
My 48ᵗʰ Birthday

Some years April 10 jerks us backwards toward winter. It can be blustery, damp and cold. But sometimes, albeit infrequently, it's most definitely spring. The trees seem impatient to burst green. Crab apple blossoms are almost out. In 2011, April 10 was an in-between day. It was obvious that spring longed to emerge. Many of my carefully planted daffodils were pushing up out of their sleep, although snow still lingered along the edges of the lawn. There was a crisp wind, and it was only about 10 degrees Celsius.

I'd spent too long without a dog, almost six months. In my home office it was far too quiet and solitary. I was used to having Lily lying next to me when I reclined on the little sofa in front of the fire to think. Lily would demand that I talk to her and then would look trustingly at me, agreeing with everything. So I'd studied the website of the closest SPCA, and I'd seen a couple of dogs that might suit me. I'd always had bigger dogs, such as Labradors or golden retrievers. The dogs I was drawn to were Lab crosses, a couple of years old and housebroken. Using a wheelchair makes house-training a dog very difficult. I liked the thought of getting a rescue dog and giving a wonderful home to an animal who had been unlucky in the past.

When Michael came home, we got in the car and drove the half hour to the shelter. The dogs are kept in outdoor runs; the sight of a human sets them off in a cacophony of sound. It's hard to talk, pathetic to see all the homeless dogs jumping up against the fences of their runs. The volunteers brought out the dogs I'd seen on the website. They seemed fine, but there was none of the elusive attraction that I felt I should sense when adopting a dog.

"Come over here! Look at this one"! Michael was crouched next to a pen. A little blonde dog of indeterminate breeding sat silently in her cage, observing the others who were all clamouring for attention.

"That's Annie. She's just been here a day. There were a whole lot of them seized from a puppy mill in London, Ontario; they've been spread across the province. Do you want to see her?" When the volunteer opened the pen, Annie ran to the back, but with the help of another volunteer, she was cornered, carried to my chair and placed on my lap. Annie trembled and shook. When I ran my hands over her, she seemed to settle a bit. My baby. After 15 minutes, a volunteer took her away. I announced that I would be back on Monday.

On Monday, I took my mother to see Annie. When they put her on my lap, she again shook with fear. As before, when I slowly ran my hand over her, the trembling lessened. My mother seemed prepared to accept whichever dog Michael and I felt would eventually accommodate itself to our lifestyle. My heart went out to the little dog. We arranged to have her spayed, and we picked her up a week later.

"The day" was April 17. In the back of my SUV, we put a crate and lined it with several layers of newspaper. Once in the crate, Annie proceeded to puke on the first layer of paper. We stopped so that Michael could peel it away. Then she peed on the second, so we stopped again. And then she pooped on the third. Before long we were home, Annie ours. We set up a crate in my office so she could be without the threat of human contact but she could still see me. She stayed in the crate for months. I racked my brain for another name, but Annie—no doubt Orphan Annie—the name she'd been given at the pound, stuck with her. It was obviously meant to be. Michael took her out on a leash in the mornings before he left for work and then again in the evenings for a prolonged period. Somebody, often one of my parents, came over and took her out at noon.

It took several months, but eventually I could open the door of her crate and let her out. First she explored my office. Then, venturing further afield, she mastered the house. After a while she was free outside as well, only restricted by the invisible fence I'd installed for Lily when I'd bought the property.

Annie's birthday is April 17, the day we picked her up from the local SPCA. At that time they told us that she was 9 to 11 months old. When we took her a week later to the local vet clinic, the vet said she was closer to a year and a half. So April 17 is now her *half* birthday, which we, besotted dog owners, celebrate every year.

It seems that as my experiences accumulate, time flies faster and faster.

Although I officially graduated in December 2010, the convocation ceremony was held in June 2011 at the National Arts Centre, the site for all University of Ottawa convocations. My thesis advisor couldn't attend, so I asked a huge favor of Cheryll Duquette, the professor who had been my grade 8 teacher:

"What would you think of coming to the graduation ceremony?"

"I'd be honoured. How neat would that be?" Her enthusiasm inspired me. I needed the encouragement. I wasn't keen on the evening, because I'd have to go onstage in a wheelchair. In the end, it all worked out. The eight seats that I had been allotted in Southam Hall were taken by my parents, Michael, two of my aunts and uncles, and James, the great friend from my past. Before the ceremony, we all had dinner together.

When it was my turn, I was wheeled up onto the stage. Cheryll walked up and joined the chancellor in conferring my degree. Then I was pushed to the back of the stage. My wheelchair and I were positioned at the end of a row of seats in which the other doctoral graduates were sitting while a couple of hundred students were conferred bachelor's and Master's degrees. I was unemotional, unaffected by the whole event, but I did find Cheryll Duquette's presence moving. How fortunate it was that we'd reconnected after all those years; how amazing it was that she was able to be there for me.

A few months later, I was driving through the town of Kars and past the location of Kars Public School, where Cheryll had been my teacher. I saw that the school was being torn down; soon there would only be a grass playing field for the newer school next door. I emailed Cheryll to let her know. I must say that I found it startling. The school building was gone, so I could no longer drive by it, triggering memories as I did so.

Despair

The convocation was a distraction, but I was soon as down as ever. Totally disinterested in the world around me, I was so apathetic about everything that I didn't even care whether my depression retreated or not. I returned to the sofa in front of the wood stove. In place of a fire— it was now the heat of the summer—I'd set up a fan, which blew cool, comforting air my way. My sofa and I were old friends. I had not been absent for long. This time, it was different. I felt lethargic and terribly sad, a bit as if I was drowning.

Dystonia was insisting on making its presence felt. Although I scrubbed endlessly at the wretched Dystonia, until my already painful emotions were raw and bleeding, the despicable illness wouldn't go away. The arduous, endless climb up the academic ladder didn't seem to matter anymore. I couldn't walk much at all. My right toe made a furrow, physical or emotional, on any road along which I was travelling. I sunk into my sadness until it became part of me. My *I* was now diminished, inconsequential. The *I* had become an "i." It seemed that i no longer had any choice but to cope with another life-changing loss. I was no longer significant.

Anguish and pain oozed through me as i mourned the second loss, Dystonia. It seemed just as distressing and life-altering as what i had gone through the first time with the head injury; in some ways, however, it felt harder, more painful. During the initial stages of recovery from the head injury, i had been emotionally unaware of the process of healing, the injury having compromised my cognitive processes. Eventually i had understood who I had been and who i was then. I'd finally adapted to the instant, monumental changes brought about by the head injury. But just when i had accommodated those losses, i'd had to face the insidious onset of chronic illness. I plunged down, retreating deep inside my shrinking self, almost drowning.

I also realized a hugely important reality: emotionally, i was not at all ready to work through a new loss. It seemed, however, that i had little choice.

Why me?

i drag myself up the stairs.

grabbing the banister;

i move my left leg up to the next step.

Then i force my right knee to bend and raise

that foot to set it down next to

my left foot.

i repeat the process.

Slowly, i make it up to my room,

where i burrow into my bed.

It hugs me,

comforts me.

My bed is my sanctuary;

i sink into its depth

and sleep the day away.

i am safe here.

As Dystonia relentlessly marched on, my emotional pain intensified. Albeit completely unrealistically, i hoped that the disease was just a transient that would eventually move on to seek nourishment elsewhere. Unable to avoid my anguish, i discovered depths of sorrow that had no business moving into my life. I cried often, wracking sobs that tore through my body, as i noisily searched for answers. *Why? Why me? Why now, after everything that has happened?* But there were no answers.

i feel my loss; it tears into me.
i sink into it, gasping for air,
because i have no choice.
shouldn't it go away?
no.
a loss like this
never slips away softly,
disappearing into the mist.

...

It makes its presence known.

I refused to acknowledge Dystonia, but it was there, a part of me, and it wasn't going to go away. The reality was that i couldn't emotionally deal with Dystonia; it was too much. Depressed, low and despondent, i felt my world was cloaked in dark grey. When these feelings crept in, i knew that i wasn't okay. Although i initially resisted it, my parents felt that i couldn't move toward being emotionally healthy without professional help.

(RE)ADJUSTING

Rather than getting preoccupied with treating symptoms, we need to help patients feel the feelings that have become unbearable to them and then find ways to solve [them].[18]

Putting Dystonia in Perspective

December 2011
Ottawa, Ontario

Comforting warm air floated by me when I pulled open the door to Dr. Levine's office, but it retreated quickly, recoiling from the subzero weather outside. Just inside the door, a steep, narrow flight of stairs rose up to the second floor. Taking a deep breath and grasping the railing on each side of the staircase, I started the climb. Left leg up to the next step, take the weight off my right leg, swing it up, hope my right knee bends a little, place it next to my left foot on the step. Repeat.

The tiny waiting room had just three chairs. Right on time, the inner door opened, and a small, balding man appeared.

"Claire! Nice to meet you. Come ahead in." Dr. Levine took his place on a chair that faced two others. On the small table in between them rested a box of tissues. He motioned me to sit down.

Typically, it takes months of waiting before one is able to get an appointment with a psychiatrist. Dr. Levine, however, picks the clients that pique his interest.

"How did I get an appointment to see you?"

"I only know a little about you, but what I know of your story intrigues me. I gather you've just graduated with a PhD! How great is that!"

He listened carefully as I explained to him that, while it was great, I felt an enormous sadness. The apparently "normal" feelings of loss after graduation had been exacerbated by Dystonia, which was intent on shoving its way into the foreground of my life.

"On that note, the stairs are a challenge." As I talked, he typed quickly on the laptop balanced on his knees.

"Did you see the coffee shop on the other side of the street? We can meet there instead, if you like. It's accessible. While we're there, we can have a coffee and one of their delicious cookies."

Dr. Levine continued, "I think that you used the PhD journey, unconsciously of course, to work through a lot of the emotional repercussions of your head injury and to process its impact on your life. When Dystonia came along, you pushed it aside, trying to ignore it as best you could. You'd blocked out emotionally dealing with Dystonia because acknowledging it would have gotten in the way of your PhD studies. It was much easier for you to pretend that there was nothing wrong than it would have been to face the fact that there was a problem. Basically, you used the PhD studies to process a lot of the lingering emotional impact of the head injury; however, the psychological consequences of Dystonia would have been, quite understandably, too much for you to handle.

"I sense that, in general, you're okay with the head injury. I suspect that your depression is due to Dystonia. After your successful recovery from head injury, Dystonia was a bit too much loss. I'm going to help you to confront Dystonia. You'll need to learn as much as you can about the chronic illness: its symptoms, its causes and possible treatments for it. Before you can begin to cope with the loss of movement that is at the root of your depression, I'll guide you so that you'll become able to allow yourself to mourn the loss of who you once were. Only then can you begin to incorporate Dystonia into your life. To do so, I'll encourage you to make accommodations to your lifestyle so that Dystonia can fade into its fabric."

For several months, i talked to Dr. Levine weekly. i found myself looking forward to my appointments, during which he was helping me through the process of first intellectually and then emotionally acknowledging the chronic illness. After that, i'd be ready to put

Dystonia into perspective. Dr. Levine gradually coaxed me out of the dark tunnel of depression in which i had found a dingy corner to call my own. Since my graduation, i'd needed somewhere to hide from the painful emotions and the reality that i didn't want to face.

Dr. Levine applauded my literature searches at the university library, urging me to read anything i could find. To intellectually acknowledge the chronic illness, i was trying to find an academic, medical solution for Dystonia, so i devoured the literature, anything i could read.

> There have been many
> studies, and lots of research
> has been done.
> There's an answer somewhere,
> i know there must be.
> There has got to be.
> i'm certain there is.
> i'm sure of it.
> Yup.

Why couldn't anyone figure out a cure? The more i read, the more i realized that a cure for Dystonia is not a reality for most people. According to the academic journal articles, many cases of Dystonia don't respond to the few medications available. In fact, just 20 percent of the cases improve when treated. I also read that the more severe the head injury, the longer after the injury Dystonia might creep into your life.

The psychiatrist guided me as i slowly moved away from only acknowledging the disease theoretically to feeling my loss emotionally. I felt assaulted by Dystonia, sure that it was trying to smother who i was. Despair and sadness rained down on me, pervasively coating my emotions in fear:

Okay, i acknowledge that I've got Dystonia.
Surely they've found a cure.
But they haven't, have they?
i have no choice;
i have to deal with this—You're kidding me?
Right?
You're not. Damn.
Give me time
i need to think, feel, experience
my pain.

When i
tentatively, cautiously
touch my feelings,
it's intensely
painful.
Burning embers, they
scorch my fingers.
OUCH!
Be careful!

Everyone around me seemed to understand how important it was to give me all the time i needed to process my loss. Experts talked to me, giving me gentle suggestions. They nudged me carefully in new directions, ones they hoped would help me crawl slowly out of the painful darkness that surrounded me. Shawn, the rehabilitation doctor, recommended a six-week program that had been organized by a psychologist at the hospital. It was about learning to deal with loss; it offered tools for coping with disability. I gazed around me at the others who were there. One girl had no right arm. Another used an electric wheelchair; muscular dystrophy was slowly robbing her of movement. I attended faithfully, learning deep-breathing exercises and talking with the others.

Dr. Levine gradually coaxed me out of the dark tunnel of depression in which i had found a dingy corner to call my own: i had needed somewhere i could hide from the painful reality i didn't want to face.

Slowly, and with great care, he guided me toward realizing what i could (still) do. He helped me to discover that i could live with Dystonia. i realized that life was not all bad. My "normal" had to be adjusted; it is now just different than it once was. I learned much later that he used psychiatrist Elvin V. Semrad's framework of theoretical acknowledging, emotionally experiencing and, finally, accommodating chronic illness[18] when he counselled people who had to learn to cope with it being a lasting part of their lives.

My small, beaten down *i* became an *I* again. I was proud of reclaiming my self. It had seemed to be an endless journey of loss, but finally I was okay.

> At long last
> I'm ready.
> I've put my losses in perspective.
> *Now*, movement equals
> wheelchair,
> scooter,
> stairlift,
> golf cart.

There was a time, during the years from 2011 to early 2014, when I cried every moment that I was reminded of Dystonia. I had trouble enjoying Christmas for a few years. Why was everyone so relaxed and happy? When visiting Michael's grandchildren, I was envious of their ability to live in the moment, a lovely characteristic of children that, at that time, I was unable to appreciate. As an athlete, I'd just thought of the next competition, the next horse, the future. In my uncertain world shadowed by the dark cloud of Dystonia, it was no doubt because of my past that I spent far too much time imagining my future.

It seemed to take forever before I was even close to being myself again. Finally, the darkness began to slowly peel away, allowing more and more light in. It took until the spring of 2014 before I felt that I'd be okay.

Since that time, rather than letting Dystonia define me, I've adjusted and adapted how I live so that I can do what I want to do, without always having to make concessions to the chronic illness. It used to be that whenever I had free time to spend with friends, I engaged in active socialization like skiing, running or walking. Dr. Levine helped me to understand that, although life is *Now* different than I ever expected it to be, I can be happy living my *Now*. I've finally acknowledged that I'm happy spending time doing things that aren't physically active, such as brunch, scrabble or theatre. I can still travel; I've just had to readjust how I do so.

I won't let Dystonia run my life.

Living with Dystonia
Now

Three times a week, at 6:30 a.m., I slide quietly out the door. A coffee and a smoothie await me in my van's cup-holders. Michael creates the smoothies quickly and then heads back to bed. The van rumbles awake, its windshield wipers shedding dew as I creep down the driveway. Although the early mist shrouds my surroundings, I can just make out Charles, the neighbour's cat, scampering through the ditch. Soon enough he'll be at our house, staring through the glass of the mudroom door, wishing for—expecting—some breakfast kibbles. Good luck to him. Michael refuses to feed him, saying he's mean to our kitty. Charles will have to wait for me to get home. I cradle my precious coffee. The radio is tuned to the CBC, so I can catch up on what's happening in the world during the 35-minute drive to Brockville. It's depressing stuff: Ebola, beheadings and starving polar bears.

The YMCA I'm heading toward has an inviting 25-metre indoor pool with huge windows and a soaring ceiling. It's a place where the outdoors seems to meet the indoors, just as in my office. I park in the handicapped parking and unload my portable wheelchair. Walking behind it, I guide it up the ramp and through the doors.

"Do you need some help?" A woman is walking toward me. Hair still damp, she's showered, finished her workout.

"Thanks so much for asking! I'm okay, though. Have a nice day!"

Lowering myself into the chair, I rest my braced right leg on the foot plate, leaving the left plate up. On pavement, asphalt or indoor surfaces, I'm able to propel myself in the portable wheelchair—it has four small wheels, so I can't u kick board se my hands—with my left foot. The wheelchair and I glide easily and quickly down the slippery linoleum hall.

I greet Karen at the reception desk. "Morning, Karen. Been for coffee yet?"

"Hi, Claire. Nope. Soon, though!"

I swipe my card and then roll past the gym filled with the young, able and muscular, turning finally into the change room for the handicapped.

My wheelchair is okay here. The staff are used to me. I think that they wonder what has happened when I don't turn up: I'm almost always there Monday, Wednesday and Friday mornings. I change quickly, efficiently. Towels draped over my chair, I push my way into the pool area. The lifeguards all know me; without being asked, they fetch me a pull-buoy and a kickboard from the supply cupboard.

Once in the pool, I am unencumbered by my disability; my foreign-feeling right leg works much better. It doesn't do what it's told to do when it's bearing weight on dry land. In the water, there is no weight on my foot, so my errant right leg behaves a bit more normally. Gliding through the water, I practise my strokes, pull-buoy keeping my legs together. Soon, though, I leave the pull-buoy up on the deck and push through the water, holding the kickboard in front of me, and concentrate on kicking, especially with my right leg. It's working; my massage therapist notices less and less difference between the muscles of my left and right legs.

"You beat me this morning!" Doris' eyes twinkle at me from the pool deck. Another Olympian, she's got me by more than a few years. She was swimming breaststroke on the British team in 1948, fifteen years before I was born. Who gets to the pool first in the morning? It's become our game; we take turns winning.

While I swim, I leave the disability that is trying to be part of who I am, though I haven't let it succeed, on the deck. For the next hour, I'm free. I've escaped from the life sentence Dystonia is trying its hardest to impose.

When I turn into the driveway after my swim, the sound of gravel crunching under my van's tires alerts my little dog, Annie, to my arrival home. Front paws on the sill of the office window lying straight ahead of me, she urges me to hurry with her ferocious barking. As I turn off the alarm, Annie speeds by me, barking fiercely at my van as if she's never seen it before.

Soon, all is peaceful. I write, sitting at my desk in front of my computer, Annie lying quietly behind my chair. Nose flat on the ground between two perfect paws. She keeps me company all day, every day.

At six o'clock one evening in June, my partner, Michael, wraps his arm securely around my waist as I transfer from my wheelchair to the lawn chair he's set up at the Ottawa Jazz Festival in Confederation Park. As is often the case, we're early, so we can strategically pick where we'll sit. It's quite close to the stage and only a few feet from the metal barrier that surrounds the lighting centre, so I can hold onto the railing if I have to move. By spreading out the canvas bags that were holding our chairs, Michael has saved places next to us for friends who will be joining us. The weather could not be better: 28 degrees Celsius under a clear sky. I slather on sunscreen and don my sun hat. Twisting around to look behind me a little later, I see a carpet of sunglasses sparkling back at me. It's a sold-out crowd tonight; the green of the expansive lawn is covered with every type of concert chair. The chairs almost overlap, nestling tightly together.

There's not much room left for the family we're waiting for, and the space we've reserved for them gets smaller as the concert time draws near. I extend my braced leg in front of me to take up some extra room. More people squeeze forward, edging closer to the stage. When Michael's friend, Rob, and his family finally do arrive, they set up their chairs and then save our spots so we're able to leave to get something to eat.

Michael helps me make my way over to the metal barrier. I move sideways along it, hand over hand, my legs crossing easily. It's not hard when I can grab a hand-level railing to support myself so that my feet are not bearing much weight. Michael follows with my travel wheelchair still "sleeping"—folded up, narrow. A girl is sitting along the barricade.

"I can easily move," she offers.

I tell her that it's all right: "If I fall on you, at least I have an excuse!" She laughs.

It's only been the past year or so that I've at long last figured out that 99.99 percent of people are wonderful. They relax if I smile, laugh and seem happy. Then they're eager to assist:

"I'll hold the door."

"Do you have enough room?"

"I can push you."

People almost always push the Handicapped button to open the door for me. They like laughing with me. They see that I'm happy. Then they're not afraid to approach me, to ask me if I need help.

I continue a few more feet along the barricade, and then Michael opens the wheelchair. It's a relief to finally sit down. As he pushes the wheelchair, I bump over the trampled grass until we reach the paved path where I can scoot along without his help. The pad thai from a vendor in the food court looks delicious. Michael carries the food, while I glide over to a free table. Under a large umbrella, we slurp up the noodles. I'm satiated but can't resist stopping at the lemonade stand as we make our way back to our chairs, the same way but in reverse.

When the sun finally lowers—it's almost the longest day of the year—everyone sheds hats and sunglasses, and the music starts. Although I'm always thinking and planning, imagining what might happen, it's moments like this one when I can slow my mind right down. I can *Now* peacefully sink into memories of my horses.

In July, when I visit my friends Diane and Mark in Barry's Bay, Ontario, the baseball cap that I'm wearing doesn't do much to prevent the wind from whipping through the ponytail that's sticking out beneath my cap, winding it around my sunglasses and blowing it across my face.

Reclining on the back bench of a motorboat, I'm wearing a silenced brace; it's not clunking noisily against the fiberglass hull. Instead, my braced leg lies comfortably on a vinyl cushion as the boat bumps across the waves of a lake in Algonquin Park. That leg will no doubt be striped under my essential brace, despite the sunscreen coating the exposed skin.

Yesterday I drove a couple of hours north to spend time with Diane, who was in the Master's program with me, and her husband, Mark. More than 10 years ago, in 2002 and 2003, I used to ski with Mark every Wednesday night from January to March at a hill only a half an hour away from Ottawa. That was a "before." Before I had to forcibly resume my battle with the infamous head injury of 1997. Before Dystonia wrapped me in its tentacles.

In 2001, BD (before Dystonia), I flew to the Czech Republic with Mark, Diane and another friend. Our trip coincided with the floods in Europe, and the Czech Republic was badly hit. My suitcase didn't make the connection in Frankfurt. Since the clothes I was wearing felt awfully grimy after the plane trip, Mark lent me a pair of his underwear that first day. Now we are even. He borrowed my extra pair of ski pants—he had forgotten his—during one of our skiing winters a year or two later. Although the pants' zipper strained constantly, it held its place and worked just fine.

The wind is exhilarating. I feel free.

My eyes close as I listen to the pianist Janina Fialkowska at the Ottawa Chamberfest. Dominion-Chalmers Church is a perfect venue; its unobtrusive air conditioning ensures that it's a comfortable refuge from the hot, humid August weather outside. The church is accessible, with a ramp and a dedicated washroom. However, we—Michael, my mother and I—must bring cushions when we come back next Wednesday to hear the Gryphon Trio. The pews are hard, suited to a church, not a concert. I stand for the entire 20-minute intermission, supporting myself by holding onto the pew in front of the one we have claimed. Fialkowska is alone on the stage, and she's playing from memory, from her heart.

No sheet music tonight. First, she plays Edward Grieg. Chopin flies through her fingers after the intermission.

John Beedell is at the concert. One of the participants in my PhD study, he competed at the 1958 World Championships and the 1960 Olympics in canoeing. He is now over 80 years old. When I'd seen him at the Chamberfest in the years following my data collection in 2008, he'd been riding his three-wheeled bike, just an oversized tricycle, between venues, travelling to a plethora of concerts. While I'd only managed to attend one or two concerts, John had pedalled madly between sites and been able to listen to many of the performances.

"Hi, John, great to see you! I can always count on you being at the Chamberfest. How many concerts this year?" I noticed that he was using a walker.

"I was hit by a car, so I'm not going to as many concerts. I can't ride my bike, so I have to rely on Para Transpo."

Late one afternoon in August, Michael and I whizz silently across the lawn at home in the electric golf cart that I bought last year, when my aged disability scooter finally kicked the bucket. I'd then insisted on an electric cart—they're silent, unlike the gas models. We motor quietly past the trees and shrubs that I've strategically planted on the property; clumps of greenery now lounge artistically on the grass. Importantly, the trees and shrubs don't require the care inherent to a flower bed. Everything has a way of working out. When I'd bought the lovely six-acre property in 2006 I'd had no idea that, just a couple of years later, I wouldn't be physically able to kneel or spend hours tending to a flower garden. Although I had no way of seeing into my future, I did know that I didn't want to spend my time lost in a flower bed. For years I'd watched my mother spending the whole day in her flower beds. I derive much more satisfaction from my trees; the property resembles an English park around an estate.

Centuries-old oaks and maples share the fertile soil with the shrubs and trees that I've planted since I moved here. Junipers, spireas, euonymus, hydrangeas, highbush cranberries, barberry and lilacs fill my eyes. I love ninebarks, so I've planted several. I nurture a pear tree, a flowering crab apple, a ginkgo biloba and a katsura. Three columnar oaks line the eastern edge of the driveway. The middle one is struggling, having been in the way of an ancient maple tree that suddenly came crashing down two summers ago. I'm cheering for the oak; it appears to be winning the struggle for survival. I'll give it a bit more time.

The verdant land is abundant with little bur oaks. Before they're too big, I try to transplant them. If they're more than a foot or eighteen inches in height, their taproots are too long, burrowing deeply into the soil and resisting relocation. It's then too late, too difficult. In the fall, the little oaks will have shed their leaves. I can transplant them then, but it's optimal, the experts say, if I wait until spring.

Labour Day marks the last day that I can swim before the lovely big pool at the Y closes for two weeks. With the cruise control set at 90 km/h, I zip along the familiar route. When I'm approaching North Augusta, the darkness begins to lift, although it's not yet seven o'clock.

As the sun seeps into the new day, it reveals handmade signs that have been crookedly nailed to the fence posts of a field belonging to the stable at the edge of town. The signs announce, in black permanent marker, that it's the day of the annual horse trials. Between two of the fence posts, the sagging page-wire fence has been folded back so that vehicles can drive into the field, today's parking lot. Just inside the entrance, a pile of gravel anticipates the already rutty track becoming deeper and muddier as the day wears on. The hazy images of this hour reveal that horse trailers are already lined up on the mown grass. I'm okay. I don't think anything of it. I'm on a mission to go swimming.

A couple of minutes later, I drive through the town. People are parking cars and trucks everywhere. They rest halfway up on the sidewalk, well off the road. Today, I suddenly realize, is the town's annual Labour Day celebration. Soon the main street that I'm driving along will be closed to traffic. I make a mental note to drive a different route home. People are effortlessly getting out of their vehicles. Suddenly, uninvited, my past screams painfully in my ear as I watch them nonchalantly walking along the sidewalk. *They don't realize what a gift it is to walk! They take it for granted!*

I pull over onto the gravel shoulder as soon as I can. Sobbing, I'm gulping in air, forcing too much of it down my throat, a new breath going in before the last one leaves. My chest heaves and my lungs overflow with teary air. When I close my eyes, it gets worse; my past spills messily into my present, flooding my *Now* and threatening to drown it in tears. Don McLean's classic "American Pie" is playing on the car stereo; its lyrics, "I can still remember how that music used to make me smile," form a backdrop for the carrousel of memories that projects haunting images of my horses onto the insides of my eyelids. My past has slammed into me; emotional detachment is no longer possible. Hands shaking, I phone Michael and then my parents.

After 10 minutes of weeping, I realize what has happened. An emotional memory, innocently sparked by the horse trials, pulled me back into my former life. Then, while I was thinking about this past—hauntingly, longingly, but still able to be emotionally detached—I saw people moving with legs that worked as uninjured legs do. It was too much. Although my precious past ended abruptly a long time ago, it will forever be chained to who I am *Now*. No matter how much time goes by, I will never be able to permanently leave behind the multitude of emotions that still lurk inside me. The rational part of me realizes that the innocent pairing of the events I drove past today shoved my losses into the foreground. Occurring as they did in tandem, the horse trials and the town's festivities unleashed such emotion, such despair, such distress—they set off such a torrent of feelings.

When my grounded self is once again ready to take control, I continue my journey. Although my tears have dried, most of me still feels sensitivity and longing as I remember the past. I have no idea whether I will ever be able to detach myself completely. The emotional injuries may never heal over; from time to time they may continue to release the pent-up pain when triggered, unleashing my past and letting it ooze into my *Now*.

I swim hard today, exhausting myself. By driving home the alternate route, I'm able to bypass the town's celebrations. Skirting around the edge, I still must drive right by the horse trials. I'm just fine, though, as I knew I would be.

In late September, a storm blew down the linden tree that my grandmother gave me when I bought Gilnockie in 2006. The tree seemed to have been flourishing, its branches full of thick leaves; it was at least 30 feet tall. But when it just blew over one day, suddenly and inexplicably, I saw that the interior of its trunk was riddled with holes.

Soon afterwards, I left a message on James's answering machine:

"Hi there. Call me—I want to cash in on my graduation present."

As a graduation present for my PhD, James, who had coached me all those years ago, had promised me a tree. At the time, we hadn't been able to find the type of tree that he wanted to give me, so the promise hadn't yet been fulfilled. Although it was now already three years after my graduation, I'd just lost the linden tree, so it seemed the perfect time to remind James about my graduation present.

It was pouring rain on the Thursday that James and I visited a local, very well-respected nursery to choose a tree. James gamely pushed my wheelchair through the rain, bumping me along the gravel and the mud of the paths so that we could examine the trees available. I critically assessed the assortment from a distance, commenting: "What about that one?" while James sloshed among them and asked Rob, the owner, about each one. When James finally narrowed it down, I stood up, walking unsteadily—the cane essential—through the mud and in between the trees, to critically examine the tree James had his eye on. Rob rushed to my side to support me as I wobbled on the uneven ground. James and I decided the tree would be perfect.

I've kept in contact with Betty Cooper over the years. She was the judge at my first horse show, and then she was the district commissioner of the local Pony Club. When Betty and her husband built their lovely house and barn, they planted trees among the jumps scattered in their backyard. The trees are grown now, creating a peaceful, park-like setting. Next to the house there's a building that, as a portrait and wedding photographer, Betty uses as a studio. Betty is a woman who gets things done! She's moved out of her house and into an apartment reimagined from part of her studio. Her son and daughter-in-law have moved into the house.

At the beginning of October, Betty called me. "Claire, why don't you come for lunch? I'll ask Ermine, too. I want you both to see what I've done." Ermine, a good friend, is James's wife.

Betty's apartment in her studio is lovely. A roomy kitchen area is open to the living space, out of which leads a door into the spacious bedroom. She's proud of her new home; it makes much more sense for her now than does the large house her son took over.

Although it was already October, the weather reminded of late August. Sunny and warm, there was not a cloud in the sky. After a lovely lunch in her apartment, I suggested that we check out my new boathouse.

Betty and Ermine followed me the 15 minutes it takes to drive to my house. There, they squished into my golf cart, and we silently made our way down the Mall to the Washington Monument. Bearing slightly left, we passed through the meadow, finally descending to the boathouse.

"Oh my." Betty was enchanted.

There had been a crumbling, unusable boathouse on the property when I bought the place. Permission to build a new one on the same footprint was grandfathered; otherwise, it would have been impossible to obtain a permit to build on the Rideau Canal system. It had still taken several years for the site to be inspected by officials and the construction to be completed. The design is simple: a boathouse only big enough for a canoe or small pontoon boat, with a six-foot wide deck on the outside along its southwest side, looking up into Nicholson's Locks.

The view from the boathouse deck.
Credit: Claire Smith

Across the river from the deck, there is only nature. Dark green cedar trees nestle behind the rustling beige reeds; the bright red Adirondack chairs on the deck are sharply, pleasingly in contrast. That day, there were clouds mirrored in the water; it was so clear and the water so still that I wanted to reach out and touch the reflected sky. As always, it was peaceful there. Serene. Utopian.

A half an hour into the visit, I realized that I'd forgotten my dog, so I whizzed up the path toward the house.

"Annie, Annie come!" In no time, Annie was flying across the lawn. I dropped her collar under a little oak where I always remove it: my dog knows that with the collar on, she's restricted inside the confines of the three-acre invisible fence, its boundary between the boathouse and the meadow. She jumped into the scooter beside me, and we descended silently to the boathouse.

It's taken years, but this property has become part of my life, a life which has been (re)imagined, (re)fashioned, (re-)created and adapted to the me of *Now*.

On Hallowe'en, Annie accompanied us when we headed toward Michael's daughter's house. Once there, we were greeted by his grandchildren. Penelope, age five, was dressed as a Princess—what else at that age?—and Finnian, one, was delighted to be a part of anything. Michael's son, Brian, was the Michelin man. Six feet in diameter, he bumped against us constantly. We munched on tortilla chips and salsa. I enjoyed it all but, as always, kept a bit of distance.

When I'm interacting with others, I sometimes find myself putting up an invisible barrier. I'm not sure why I do this. Am I unconsciously protecting myself from the normal, the everyday? For years, my blinkered life—it had included horses and nothing else—precluded my participation in what I considered to be normal events, the way most people spend their time. People normally meet friends for dinner at a restaurant, they make an evening out of going to the theatre or to ballet or they have fun at their book club meetings.

In my old life, these activities would never have seemed normal to me. Instead, I'd felt normal when I was striving for excellence in everything I did. I'd been relentlessly driven, dedicated and motivated. When I was still young, horses had taken over my life. Soon, excellence had been defined by me as being successful in the sport that called to me so strongly. I'd been the obsessed teenager. The blinkered young adult. Not only before the infamous accident of 1997 but also for many years after, excellence had meant reaching the pinnacle, being the best at what I did. For me, it was normal to constantly strive for excellence. When I could no longer ride, achieving academic excellence became my raison d'être. Excellence was black and white: either you were or you weren't. I think that's the way most people would describe excellence.

However, the years spent recovering (first from the head injury and later from Dystonia) and then the years after the PhD have, at long last, changed my notions of *normal* and *excellence*. Do I still strive for excellence? Absolutely. Excellence, however, means a lot more than it used to. In the past, excellence was only about me, how I measured up to others. Life was a competition.

It's taken me far too long to realize that excellence is something that can't be evaluated or scored. Excellence is still doing my best, but its outcome is not quantifiable. I've come to realize that excellence has a lot to do with how I feel about myself. Although excellence comes from within myself, it's *Now* not just about me. It's about feeling good after giving to and helping others. It's about doing things for and with others.

In mid-November, I have an appointment at the Ottawa Hospital Rehabilitation Centre to have my brace adjusted. It's just five minutes from Fran and Ken's new apartment, so I called Fran a couple of days ago to suggest that we meet for a coffee when I'm done.

During the MA journey, I'd often found myself driving to Fran and her husband, Ken's, house in the suburbs of Ottawa. Sometimes I'd picked Fran up at her home and we'd gone for dinner, Italian some nights, fish others. We'd chatted about her teaching and my climb toward an MA and then a PhD. Other times, I'd brought lunch and we'd eaten together in her sunny breakfast room. In 2007 Fran had stopped teaching; her Parkinson's had advanced to the point that she no longer felt cognitively able to prepare for and lead a class. Then our conversations had drifted into how we were coping with our respective disabilities. At the time, I'd been facing a new demon; Dystonia was trying its hardest to take over my right leg.

Although it's been a few years since I graduated, I still stay in touch with Fran. We've become friends, enjoying each other's company and talking about all sorts of things. In 2014, all too aware of the progression of Fran's disease and in order to simplify their lives, Fran and Ken moved to a large apartment close to the same neighbourhood in which they had lived for the past 20 years.

While chatting—then in her house, and now in her apartment—Fran and I are usually caught in the moment, in the *Now*, swirling together stories about academics, our disabilities and where we feel we currently belong. We recognize that we are forever evolving in a world that doesn't stand still. Instead, it moves on relentlessly, carrying us and our respective disabilities with it. Sometimes our talk drifts toward the future. There are many people gathered under the umbrella of disability. I'm all too aware that, at least until today, I'm one of the better-off ones.

The path of Dystonia is unknown—will it invade more of my body? I remain thankful that to date it has not. Beneath this ever-present cloud of uncertainty, I choose to be optimistic, thankful that Dystonia has stayed put in my right leg. Fran, however, is less optimistic; she's noticing the relentless advancement of Parkinson's.

Since about 2010, I've worn a brace to stop my leg from painfully bending backwards when I stand on it. I swim without the brace on; I sleep without the brace on; I sit normally at my desk. In each of these cases, there is no weight against the bottom of my right foot. But the instincts in my right leg are so strong that when I stand on it, my brain tells my leg to fight against the brace, and it tries in vain to straighten itself. Over the course of several months, because my leg pushes constantly against it, the brace gives imperceptibly. Given enough time, my leg starts to win the battle. Eventually, the brace is bent just enough so that my leg hyperextends to the point that my right knee feels as if it's ever so slightly bending backwards—just where

Dystonia wants it to be. Then I make an appointment with Ted, an orthotist at the rehabilitation centre.

The prosthetics and orthotics clinic is a godsend. I'd never heard of an orthotist before I needed a brace for my leg. Orthotists design, fabricate and fit braces or splints, with the intent of preventing or correcting deformities, or making a deformity less painful. By improving the function of a weakened extremity, customized braces designed by orthotists help people with physical deformities function optimally in their everyday lives. In my case, Ted had designed a couple of braces for my leg over the last few years. To customize the braces, he'd first wrapped my leg in a quick-drying plaster. Slicing the plaster open once it was dry provided him with a mould of my leg, which he then used to fashion my custom brace.

It was incredibly cold out when I left Merrickville at 7:30 in the morning to drive to the other end of Ottawa for my 9:00 appointment. Covered only by his dressing gown, Michael came out to the car with a coffee and then quickly ducked back inside the warm house, followed by the dog. I knew that they were both headed upstairs to crawl back into their respective beds. Thank God for heated car seats! Before long, although my breath was still visible as it curled around me in the freezing-cold car, my bum was toasty.

In the waiting room, my fingers gradually thawed as I cuddled a coffee. Clients with amputated limbs and using an endless assortment of custom devices came and went. I was always amazed and fascinated. People with leg amputations—their lower leg gone, or a whole leg missing and every level in between—learned to walk with prosthetic limbs. Soon, anyone watching wouldn't be able to tell that they no longer had the legs they'd been born with.

My appointment lasted an hour. I asked Ted, the orthotist, about his daughters. They were aged three and five; I remembered when he'd taken parental leave at their births. It was frightening, not only because time seemed to fly but because I'd started seeing him before number one had arrived.

As my Dystonia has progressed, Ted has built me a series of braces.

The one I wear *Now*, which I've had for about three years, covers my entire right leg. I'm so dependent on it that, after two years, when my insurance would pay for a second, I had him design a new one that is exactly the same. In case something happens, brace number two will always be there as a backup.

Fran and Ken's new apartment is so close to the General that when I called from my car and Ken answered, he teased me: "Oh, I see your car just pulling out onto Smythe Road."

"I'll be there in five. Ask Fran to get bundled up and come down. I'll pick her up at the back door."

Within five minutes, Fran was in the car, and I drove to the local coffee shop. Fran and I talked about her week-long visit to Toronto, a trip to see Ken's sister and their old friends.

We didn't discuss Parkinson's or Dystonia. Perhaps we should have. When we were standing at the cash to pay before we left, my newly adjusted brace shot pain up my leg. Fran, ever aware, noticed my discomfort and told me to go sit in the van. I did so, but when Fran walked over, cradling a box of lemon tarts, she opened the passenger door and fell as she tried to negotiate the curb, the pavement and the made-much-more-difficult-by-a-snowbank climb into my van. The box flew through the air, landing upside down in the snowbank. Lemon curd splattered colourfully onto the dirty snow.

"Fran! Are you all right?" I didn't believe what I'd just seen.

"The third time this week! That's it, then." I was not so sure it was, as closely tuned as I was to the progression of Fran's disease. Maybe that was because it reflected the anxiety I felt about the possible progression of mine—but it was definitely because she's a great person and a treasured friend.

When I consider the emotional anguish that I went through before I made peace with Dystonia, it's clear that the following email exchange would perplex me. In late 2015, an article was published that I'd submitted to an academic journal a year and a half earlier.[19] In it, I discuss that the way in which I have chosen to live my life in the presence of chronic illness is a departure from the expected "acceptance of disability." Instead, I continue to view Dystonia as an unwelcome presence that has tried to take over my life. Dystonia will always be part of me, but I don't believe that I'm characterized by my disability. I'm not "confined" to a wheelchair; instead, I "use" a wheelchair.

In her/his comments, one of the reviewers mentioned that the article made her/him question disability and its relationship to identity. She/he obviously was still grappling with the concept when I got her/his second comments after I had resubmitted it with extensive revisions. The reviewer wrote that it had stretched her/his thinking to see Dystonia "in more of a duality than I'm sure is a reality for some." I still think about that comment. For me, it flew in the face of how I've learned to live my life, how I've tried to put my loss—Dystonia—in perspective. Although it will always be part of my identity, I'll always consider it a duality. Yes, I have Dystonia. At the same time, however, I am so many other things and I have so many other qualities.

On the morning of December 19, I bugged Michael, as I do every day, until he walked out to get the newspaper. Although November had been miserable, December thus far has been mild. Today though, the weather taunted him to dress more warmly. He unenthusiastically made his morning trek to the end of the driveway.

Part of my routine, when Michael brings me the paper, is to read the death notices. That day, I was shocked to see a familiar photo. John Beedell, one of the participants in my PhD study, had died. When I'd interviewed him in 2008, he'd been 75 years old. He'd been fit and game for life, and his bright eyes had welcomed our sessions. Saddened, I knew I would miss seeing his expressive face. I fondly remember the lovely chats we'd had about his interesting life.

My parents took thirteen of us—almost everyone in our immediate family—to Quebec City, where we spent the 21st, 22nd and 23rd of December at the Chateau Frontenac. The only one missing was number fourteen—my partner, Michael. Retail is all-important in the days before Christmas.

Glistening ice-coated trees decorating our drive, my parents and I crossed the St. Lawrence River on the new toll bridge west of Montreal. Once over the bridge, we were surrounded by remote suburbs and farmers' fields as we made our way east, gliding uninterrupted around the city on Highway 30. Continuing along the south shore of the river and then crossing the river again just west of Quebec City, we arrived at the Chateau Frontenac in the late afternoon.

My brother John had scheduled the dining arrangements and made reservations. We spent the first night devouring crêpes. The next morning, after breakfast overlooking the St. Lawrence, my history-buff father led the way. We visited the Citadel on the 22nd and then old Quebec City the next morning. In a museum in the Old City, we donned period costumes and posed for a plethora of photos. Christmas or New Year's cards, perhaps? That afternoon we discovered an indoor market, its snowless paved walkways easy for me to navigate. The market proved to be very useful for purchasing Christmas presents. On the walk back to the Chateau, my two brothers took turns pushing me uphill and through the snow; it was instant exercise for them. As we made our way back through old Quebec City, my imagination was easily lit by huge snowflakes that were softly falling, sprinkling even more Christmas atmosphere over the tastefully wreathed and bowed old stone buildings. *Who lived here many centuries ago?* I wondered. *How did they live?* When the light began to fade around four in the afternoon, the Christmas lights twinkled even brighter as we caught the funicular up to the Chateau.

It seems to have taken forever, but finally I've reached the point where I don't think much about my wheelchair. Using one has made my life workable for me. But the attendant at the base of the funicular, without once looking at me, said to my brother, who was pushing the wheelchair, "You can push her around the turnstile by going around the barrier to the left."

Once in the funicular, I swivelled around to talk to John Willem and said, "It happens very rarely that someone will completely ignore me, talking instead to whoever is pushing the wheelchair. The individual, I think, believes that the wheelchair means that I'm compromised, that I can't think for myself, that I'm not a real person."

"I get it now." He nodded, finally seeing my reality for himself. At one time, some individuals' assumptions when they see a person using a wheelchair bothered me a lot. That I was no longer affected by their presumptions revealed how far I'd travelled along my healing journey. I'd learned that these reactions were not about me as a person. To the odd person, I'm invisible, but the wheelchair is not.

When we headed home on Christmas Eve morning, we longed for the same snowflakes that we'd witnessed on our drive there, but instead, rain splattered the windshield. The snow on the fields dissolved before our eyes, and the sparkling trees of our drive down were only memories, both victims of a premature January thaw. Much later, I marvelled at the coincidence of the vanished snow: it effectively symbolized that my feelings of invisibility when using my wheelchair had melted away. *Now,* I'd healed to the point that, however people might react to me, I no longer felt invisible when I was sitting in my wheelchair.

Now

Early April
Merrickville, Ontario

Unbelievably, it snowed last night. There's enough that hasn't melted that Michael might have to shovel when he gets home, a winter chore that I can no longer do. I can't say I miss it. Shovelling walkways was never my favorite pastime.

I've come to terms with the brace that covers my whole leg. But although I'm now all right with my compromised lifestyle, I might never be okay with feeling imprisoned during these winter months. I used to dislike— hate—some aspects of winter. I loved downhill skiing, but I hated it when my frozen fingers, white with frostbite, became red, hurting like crazy until, achingly, slowly, they thawed and returned to normal. I used to have to painfully peel my neck warmer off my face. Although I'd pulled it up until it was under my googles, so that my nose was covered, my breath often froze the neck warmer in place.

I long for that discomfort, that pain, because I'll never again experience its cause. I miss winter sports a lot.

I didn't have a clue about disability all those years ago. I'm embarrassed to admit how long it took me to open my eyes to the compromises that so many individuals must make in what they do and how they do things, because they have no choice but to accommodate their disabilities. As someone who didn't live with disability and wasn't close to someone with a disability, I had no idea what it was all about. It didn't impact me or anyone I knew well, so why would I know? I wonder now how I could have been so unaware of all the people who, because they are forced to come to terms with illness or disability, have no choice but to consider it when choosing how to live their lives.

In no way did I mean to be oblivious—I just had no idea what it was all about until I became one of them.

A New Year

2016

The cruel Canadian winter was flourishing in the middle of January 2016 when Michael and I left it behind to fly to Naples, Florida, to join my long-time friend James for a week in its restorative warmth. A rental car took us on the 40-minute drive to Naples.

Dystonia has necessitated that the notion of freedom of movement is completely different than I'd ever imagined it would be. In Naples, I silently cruised the neighbourhood on my rented electric scooter, while James and Michael walked. At the end of every day, shortly after six in the evening, the sidewalk would zip beneath my scooter while James and Michael hurried along beside me on our three-block journey to the beach. We were not the only ones to head to the pier to catch the setting sun; it seemed that many houses in Naples offered their occupants to the sinking sun. We watched as, regular as clockwork, the sun disappeared into the sea, closing another day.

In late December 2015, I'd tempted Michael with tantalizing stories of sunshine and 75-degree weather until he promised to accompany me to Texas, where I was heading in February 2016 to present at a conference. In the middle of February, Michael and I flew to the supposed warmth of Texas. However, when the plane landed in San Antonio, it was chilly. It was so cold that I was grateful to have packed a light winter jacket and gloves—"just in case." The next day, although there was not a cloud to be seen, the temperature was still below normal. The scenery delighted us as Michael pushed me along the Riverwalk. Outdoor restaurants sprinkled the river's edge with colourful table umbrellas, Mexican tiles were everywhere and palm trees abounded. We took a taxi out to the San Juan Mission and marvelled at its size and its history.

After picking up the rental car on Thursday afternoon, we headed west toward San Angelo. Just 10 miles from our destination, the boring, softly rolling scrubland that we'd endured for the past couple of hours became flat and prairie-like. Huge lush, verdant fields, stretching far into the horizon, filled our eyes. Long irrigation pipes, dipping like empty clotheslines between huge support wheels, marched across immense acreages. During these winter months, they lie motionlessly waiting, poised to quench the earth's thirst when summer's extreme heat arrives.

Friday morning, everything outside the hotel room window sparkled. Freezing rain had coated the world. Before we slithered off to the conference, Michael discovered that scraping the ice off the windshield of our rental car, normally not an issue, had become one. No car in Texas is equipped with a scraper and brush, an item found in all cars in Canada. Michael did his best with the edge of a credit card, and finally we climbed into the rental and cautiously proceeded toward Angelo State University. Spreading salt and sand is unheard of this far south, so the roads were treacherous. We were nervous of the other cars that were inching along the slippery roads. In all likelihood, their drivers had little or no experience in such icy conditions.

After a harrowing drive, we finally arrived at the university. However, I feared that I might be stuck in the car all day. It was almost impossible to gain any grip at all when I tried to stand on the icy pavement. Michael slithered my wheelchair across the glare ice until I only needed to stand and then rotate 90 degrees to sit in it. But when I grabbed hold of the car door and tried to cautiously hoist myself upright, my summery shoes only slipped and slid on the ice. It took several attempts until, finally, I ungraciously plopped into my wheelchair. Although I breathed a huge sigh of relief—*I've made it!*—I realized that, despite all our travails, it wasn't yet eight in the morning. We seemed to have already dealt with our share of problems, but the reality was that the day had not yet started.

Safely inside the building, sheltered from the icy outdoors, I pushed myself silently between rooms. I was to do two presentations that day, the first an excerpt from this book, the second an exploration of why I was writing it. Academia swirled around me. Soon though, I found myself saturated, overloaded with discussions of studies and research. To my surprise, I realized that I didn't care about everything—anything— that was happening at the conference. People spoke passionately when they talked about their research, but I wasn't listening. I wasn't engaged or interested; I wasn't questioning the speakers.

Mired in an academic world that I'd assumed was the next step along my journey, I suddenly realized that it wasn't for me. At long last it became apparent to me that academia itself didn't inspire me. Although I'd felt enormous relief when I'd graduated with a PhD, it was finally dawning on me that since then I'd been unconsciously struggling with the question of what I should do next, who I should be.

Several years after attaining a PhD, the twofold purpose of my return to academia a long 15 years ago suddenly became clear to me—working toward an MA and then a PhD degree had been important parts of my healing journey. For both degrees I had explored the impact that head injury had had on me and how it had affected others who had sustained similar injuries.

Finally, it all made sense. I'd been ensnared by this past for too long. It was time to move on, time to find another journey to embark on. Although I believe that I'll never reach the end of my healing journey, I finally felt that I had it in sight. I *Now* felt ready to cut free from it all—no more research or writing about head injury and no more academic conference presentations. I still have a constant stream of speaking engagements dotting my calendar. I'll still speak about my experiences of head injury and chronic illness, but I'll do so in non-academic environments.

There's another, equally important, reason why I pursued the degrees. Working toward the MA and the PhD provided me with goals, as had my equestrian past. However, I was surprised when I discovered that the time I spent working toward my MA and PhD—unlike the time I'd spent on my purpose-oriented undergraduate degree—was as much about the *journey* toward the degrees as it was about attaining the goals. The friends made, the non-academic lessons learned and my increased knowledge about others' healing experiences after head injury meant as much to me as the degrees themselves.

I finally understood the twofold purpose of my return to academia. First, going back to university after the head injury had facilitated my processing of that life-changing event. Doing so enabled me to wrest myself out of that difficult past and to move out of the shadow of head injury; I'd made friends who had no preconceived ideas about me. Second, university provided me with a goal. Importantly, while I was a student the second time around, I learned to let myself enjoy the journey toward both the degrees.

At long last, I understood the real reasons behind my academic journey.

Michael and I rented a house in Sedona, Arizona, for the month of March 2016. Once a voracious skier, since Dystonia struck I've felt imprisoned by the Canadian winter. I'm trapped inside by the cold, snowy and/or icy conditions outside, which are made more treacherous by my braced leg.

In Sedona, however, the March weather is always marvellous. Seventy-five degrees Fahrenheit and dry is usual. The incredible view from our deck is amply embellished with the area's red sandstone hills. I was outside every possible minute, feeling free at last. My days were spent lounging on the deck, wearing lots of sunscreen and a large hat. Because my brace was off my leg the whole time that I was lying on the deck, the sun slowly bronzed the pale stripes it had left on my skin; the patchwork appearance all but disappeared. The brace's nearly constant presence—both emotionally and physically—became invisible at long last.

Friends from different parts of my life joined us. For the past few years, Fran, my first professor along my MA journey, and her husband, Ken, have spent February and March in Sedona. Anne, my great friend who had ridden my horse Master Sing many years ago, and her husband, Andrew, flew from North Carolina to join us for a week.

The men hiked most mornings, while Anne and I lazed in the sun, novels at the ready. I'd known Anne since the late 1980s; we'd been introduced after both being recruited to develop an equine program for a community college close to home in Canada. Even though Anne and Andrew had moved to South Carolina more than two decades ago, we'd always stayed in touch. Old friends, we fell easily into conversation, so we accomplished little reading.

"Boy, I remember September 13, 1997, even if you don't," said the sunhat from the next chaise lounge. Anne's abundant red hair peeked out from underneath it. She recounted a story that I'd heard many times:

> At 10 p.m., my husband, Andrew, and I were wrapped up cozily in our sleeping bags, lying in the peak of my two-horse gooseneck trailer. I was competing your horse Master Sing at an event in Blythewood, South Carolina. After everything was done for the day, we'd spent the half hour before bedtime sitting on lawn chairs outside the trailer, enjoying a couple of glasses of wine with friends who were also competing. Master Sing had luxurious accommodations in the temporary stabling tent just a short walk across the field.
>
> Someone knocked loudly on the trailer door.
>
> "Andrew, if someone wants a glass of wine, we have no more." I pulled the sleeping bag over my head and pretended that I was fast asleep.
>
> The trailer door swung open. "Thought you needed to know—we don't know any of the details, but Claire has had an accident on the cross-country course at

Burghley, in England. It's really bad. I'm sorry to tell you that they're not sure if she'll make it."

I was suddenly wide awake—horrified, disbelieving and panicky. Fumbling in the dark, I found my jeans and a T-shirt. Stumbling across the field to the stabling tent, I slipped on Sing's halter. His eyes blinked; he was not at all pleased that I'd disturbed his beauty rest. Luckily, he loved grass. The two of us wandered the field. I hugged him lots, but he was in the moment and just wanted to be left alone to graze.

"Luckily, I don't remember a thing from that day. Sorry to have been the cause of such stress!"

While Anne and Andrew were there, we had dinner with Fran and Ken a couple of times, first at our house and then at theirs. I quietly observed these good friends from very different periods of my life, brought together in a place foreign to us all. Fran and I have known each other for 15 years now; we're amazed when we realize how much time has elapsed since we met. She has, entirely unwillingly, been captured by Parkinson's. I notice that the disease has progressed, albeit slowly. Anne is still ensnared by the life that I left behind a long time ago. Despite being on vacation, she regularly gets texts from her equestrian clients. Then there's me. I *Now* feel free. I'm finally able to put Dystonia in its place.

Now

April 11
Gilnockie

The robbed that smiles steals something from the thief.
—William Shakespeare, *Othello*

The fire in the wood stove sparkles and dances from the corner of my office, belying the lingering winter outside. Although I find it impossible not to miss the much warmer weather of Arizona and Texas, I'm enchanted as I gaze through the window at six o'clock in the evening, mesmerized by the light as it slowly fades away, the sky relinquishing its daytime grip to the night. Muted orange skies sink behind the trees edging my still snow-patched lawn, skies that will soon disappear into the earth.

Watching the sunset is one of my favourite things to do during the drawn-out winter months. Only in the past couple of years have I realized how fulfilling it is to sculpt my precious past, and my *Now*, into words. It's taken almost all the years since that fateful September 13 for me to learn how to embrace the moments that are happening *Now*, how to hold them close and refuse to let them go until I can slide them from my mind into my computer. Time can't touch them there. I can quietly enjoy them because they'll *Now* live forever.

This book came to be because I finally realized that, if I wanted to understand not just how to live in the *Now* and survive, but how to enjoy each moment, I had to revisit my horses, a most beloved time of my past. It was essential to my emotional health that I work through those precious memories. By doing so, I was able to "lift the lid off my life and inspect what was contained."[20] Writing about those memories, those times has, at long last, enabled me to tuck my cherished life with my horses peacefully away. *Now*, I'm okay when I revisit that time. It seems to have taken me forever to realize that I don't crave what that past was, what I was, anymore. For a long time, I constantly longed for who I used to be: desperately clutching at memories of that beloved life, hopelessly idealizing what my life would have been like if that magical time had evolved into a future.

Although I no longer openly acknowledge September 13, the day arrives yearly with clockwork regularity. It tries to taunt me with haunting memories and harrowing stories of the first years after I was injured. I used to actively hide from these stories that I had convinced myself were bent on etching and staining me. I refused to acknowledge that I owned these tumultuous times. I dodged these memories as much as I could: tough, weighty memories, reminders of a time I was forced to spend in transition between lives. During that time in limbo, before I had found a new direction, I spent an inordinate amount of time avoiding eye contact with the identity shoved upon me by the head injury.

At long last, I'm able and ready to do as Behar (1996) suggests: bring my past into the present so I can experience not only what I have lost, but also what and who I am despite this loss.[21] I can close my eyes and (re)visit my past because going there in my thoughts no longer disturbs me, nor do my thoughts of that past try to venture imaginatively into an unattainable future. I don't want to live the rest of my life constantly, achingly and longingly revisiting, recalling and re-examining life as it once was. So, I've chosen to live *Now*.

One of the most important lessons that I took away from my university years is that everyone has a plurality of identities. For the first 34 years of my life, a singular, narrow and extremely focused equestrian identity defined—confined—me. Until September 13, 1997, I'd refused to contemplate that I was anything but a rider. When I finally came to terms with the reality that my equestrian life was over, that identity was over too. It was extremely hard for me to process the loss of Claire the equestrian. I couldn't imagine being anything but a rider, so I'd shut my mind to the endless opportunities available to me.

University was the perfect opportunity to latch onto another singular identity: I became a student. When I graduated, that identity was no longer, so I was lost yet again. Eventually, I realized that I needed to apply to myself what I'd learned during my time at university: everyone has a plurality of identities. Considering that I'd spent several years researching and learning about identity(ies), it took far too long for me to open my eyes and realize that I'd been repressing countless identities of my own.

My awakening, my realization of all the identities that are part of me, has led me to live an inspired and diverse life filled with friendships, evenings out at the ballet, theatre, book club, gardening and so much more. Most of the old friendships from my equestrian life have faded away; I've moved on, as I'm sure they have. New friends now call, email and knock on my door. My world has expanded exponentially and I've become a richer and more interesting human being.

Today, I believe that I evolve daily, always welcoming change and new experiences, continually creating new identities, constantly resculpting me. One of these identities is central: I'm a writer. I can, at long last, painlessly create stories from my memories. Writing has become an inextricable part of me, one with which Dystonia can't interfere.

When I finally emerged from the dark cloud of Dystonia, I realized that even if I was physically well, my life would need to be continually retuned. The momentous event that will forever colour my life occurred over 19 years ago. It took me many years to realize that my 1997 fall had altered me enormously, permanently. I was well on the way to healing the silent and harmful emotional damage the injury had left in its wake when, several years after the fall, the chronic illness Dystonia re-infected those psychological wounds. It was much worse the second time around but the wounds have now scarred and are rock solid under my emotional feet. Although I can now dance through life, I realize that the wounds may fester again if given the opportunity, once again becoming unchecked. Dangerous. Only time will reveal if the healing is but tenuous.

The physical aspects of Dystonia insidiously mark me; they've made the head injury visible to all. I did not expect that being visibly disabled would become a fixture of my evolving identity: does anyone, ever? I certainly didn't want it to be. The wheelchair underlines my disability: it is an artifact that makes public my injury. It's far too easy to make assumptions about someone who is using a wheelchair. A wheelchair is immediate: it's "in your face." For a long time, I felt defined by my wheelchair; now there's no way I'd let it define me. I'm not confined to it either. I use it.

Wheelchair = movement

Using a wheelchair just means that my "normal" is different than it once was. For me, normal means adapting to my losses and accommodating them. Normal is driving a van—I thought until a year ago that vans symbolized suburban motherhood—equipped with a wheelchair lift. I am completely independent. Normal is living comfortably in an old stone house, in which I installed a stair lift to reach the second floor. Normal means that instead of strolling around my wonderful property, I drive an electric golf cart so I can enjoy it fully. I've learned to live in new, forward-thinking ways that were once unimaginable. I've taken illness and disability, normally seen as negatives, and turned them on their heads, so that for me they are now positives.

I glide through life once more: metaphorically, emotionally and physically. I sometimes use the wheelchair lift in my van, but most of the time my portable wheelchair with its small wheels skates me to where I want to go. Pushing along a smooth floor with my able left foot propels the chair at a pace faster than a brisk walk. I have fashioned my life so that I feel one and the same as able-bodied others. I don't believe that I have let Dystonia carve me into pieces. I despise Dystonia with all my heart, so I'm not going to let it dictate how I live. Dystonia will always lurk menacingly in my life's shadows, but I refuse to give it the satisfaction of letting its presence affect me, even though the wheelchair makes its consequences visible to all. Sure, life would be a lot easier without Dystonia as part of it, but at long last, I've left behind the emotional anguish that Dystonia once was.

It's taken years since that fateful September 13 of 1997, but I finally feel settled, content … happy. It's taken me seemingly forever to understand what I need to do next: I need to find another goal to work toward, another journey to embark on. I'm still extremely focused. However, I've learned that when I work toward my next goal, whatever it may be, by fully experiencing the journey, I'll be contributing to my never-ending quest to discover who I am *Now*. At long last, I'm living in the moment. By relishing the present, I can bask in today instead of mourning the past. Finally, I can peacefully imagine the unknown future.

Soon, Michael will come home. He finds it peaceful, relaxing, to cook both of us a delicious dinner. Before he returns, as the setting sun shutters for the night, I wheel over to my desk to write. I'm finally at peace with myself.

I am okay *Now*,
even better than I used to be.
I see, I smell, I hear, I feel
everything around me.
At long last, I finally
appreciate the person inside,
the one Dystonia can't touch:
me.
The one who is
alive—*Now*.

The thief Dystonia may have robbed me of movement, but I've learned how to smile again.[22]

Acknowledgments

I couldn't possibly have composed this memoir without the help and support of many people. You talked with me, listened to me and read for me. Thank you, my friends; your support has been tremendous.

When I enrolled in the Humber School for Writers Correspondence Program in creative writing in 2012, I worked with Sandra Birdsell while composing the first draft. In that early version, people who I'd met at various times in my life told me their stories. I thank Sandra for her thoughtful suggestions. My friends Glennis Easey, Rosanne Dawson, Sandra Kelly, Fran Squire and James Wright shared stories about their lives. Although the book's format has changed dramatically, you all still play parts in the published version. I thank you for your patience as I worked through many drafts.

Humber College set up a chat room for students enrolled in the course. Carmelita Boivin-Cole, who I met in that chat room, has become a good friend. Thank you for not just being there but continuing to read and comment on my work. I love our Skype conversations!

A year later, when I enrolled in the Humber course again, I worked with Karen Connelly, who persuaded me not to hide behind the stories of others when telling my own story. I had to start all over again, but in the end, I thank Karen for her counsel. Also, thank you to Antanas Sileika, who was the director of the program at the time. He helped me a couple of years after the course ended when I was first trying to publish this book.

A big thanks to Betty Cooper, who I've known for many years.

Now a photographer, she tinkered with a couple of old photos so that I could use them in the book. It took a bit of searching to find the current contact information for photographers who took pictures at least twenty years ago, when I was riding. Thank you to Julie Siegel, VW Perry Photographic and Terri Miller for giving me permission to use your photos and for showing such interest in the book. Lianne and Roger Sands of Arranel Studios took the author photo. Thank you, I love it.

To Liz Mills Campbell, Ronalee Carey, Leni Harubin, BJ Reid, Judith Robertson, Leanne Mundy, Lianne Sands and Wendy Quarry, all friends from very different parts of my life, many thanks for thoughtfully commenting on various drafts of the manuscript. A big thanks to Peri Howlett and Anne Maunder, who thoroughly edited earlier versions. Thanks to Facebook, I'm reacquainted with a friend from years ago—when we were both seven! Karyn Curtis works as an editor and, as well as chatting with me on the boathouse deck, read and edited the manuscript several times. Thank you very much—I'm so happy to have found you! I'm terrified that I've forgotten to thank somebody; my sincere apologies if that is the case.

Lastly, a huge thanks to my parents: you've made it possible for me to be who I am *Now*. To my partner, Michael, thank you so much for understanding me *Now* and putting up with me when I can't seem to leave my computer—it happens often. Finally, a big hug for Annie. You listen to me with rapt attention, your ears pricked and your eyes wise. Just the audience I need when I'm bouncing ideas around; I know you don't understand a word I'm saying.

Endnotes

[1] A. Frank, *The Wounded Storyteller: Body, Illness, and Ethics* (Chicago: the University of Chicago Press, 1995), p. 76.

[2] L. Richardson and E. Adams St. Pierre, *Writing: A Method of Inquiry*, In Y. Lincoln and N. Denzin (eds.), *The Sage Handbook of Qualitative Research*, 3rd ed. (Thousand Oaks, California: Sage Publications, 2005), p. 967.

[3] A. Frank, *At the Will of the Body: Reflections on illness* (New York: Houghton Mifflin Company, 2002), p. 1.

[4] J. Didion, *Blue Nights* (New York: Random House, 2011), p. 13.

[5] Mia Hamm, retired American professional soccer player.

[6] http://olympic.ca/canadian-olympic-committee/values/.

[7] Ibid.

[8] A. Frank, *The Wounded Storyteller: Body, Illness, and Ethics*, p. 102.

[9] NRI Neurologic Rehabilitation Institute at Brookhaven Hospital, http://www.traumaticbraininjury.net/.

[10] Y. Su, A. Veeravagu, and G. Grant, *Neuroplasticity after Traumatic Brain Injury*, In D. Laskowitz and G. Grants (eds.), *Translational Research in Traumatic Brain Injury* (Boca Raton, Florida: CRC Press/Taylor and Francis Group, 2015), pp. 163–178.

[11] http://www.traumaticbraininjury.net/outcome-studies/.

12 T. M. McMillan, E.L. Jongen, and R. J. Greenwood, "Assessment of post-traumatic amnesia after severe closed head injury: retrospective or prospective?" *Journal of Neurology, Neurosurgery & Psychiatry* 60 (1996): pp. 422–427.

13 Y. Kosch, S. Browne, C. King, G. Fitzgerald, and I. Cameron, "Post-Traumatic Amnesia and Functional Outcome After Brain Injury," *Brain Injury* 24, 3 (2010): 479–485.

14 M. Konigs, J. de Kievet, and J. Oosterlaan, "Post-traumatic amnesia predicts intelligence impairment following traumatic brain injury: a meta-analysis," *Journal of Neurology, Neurosurgery & Psychiatry* (2012).

15 A. Frank, *The Wounded Storyteller: Body, Illness, and Ethics*, p. 77.

16 C. Osborn, *Over My Head: A Doctor's Own Story of Head Injury from the Inside Looking Out* (Kansas City, Missouri: Andrew McMeel Publishing, 1998), p. XII.

17 A. Frank, *The Wounded Storyteller: Body, Illness, and Ethics*, p. 117.

18 S. Adler, and M. Day, "Learning to do psychotherapy with psychotic patients: In memory of Elvin Semrad, M.D," 2010, retrieved August 31, 2015, from http://www.rheumatologynetwork.com/schizophrenia/learning-do-psychotherapy-psychotic-patients-memory-elvin-semrad-md.

19 C. Smith, "(Re)imagining 'normal' movement: Dystonia, the chronic illness disrupting my life," *Departures in Critical Qualitative Research* 4, 3 (2015): 92–107. doi: 10.1525/dcqr.2015.4.2.92.

20 R. Wagamese, *Indian Horse*, (Madeira Park, British Columbia: Douglas & McIntyre, 2012), p. 207.

21 R. Behar, *The Vulnerable Observer: Anthropology that Breaks your Heart*, (Boston, Massachusetts: Beacon Press, 1996).

22 The opening *Now* and the closing *Now* contain passages previously published in endnote #19.

About the Author

Credit: Arranel Studios

Claire Smith is the author of several articles published in academic journals and has spoken at many academic and nonacademic events. A board member of the Wings of Phoenix, whose mandate it is to raise funds for survivors of head injury, she is also a member of the Leeds and Grenville Accessibility Advisory Committee, and is on the board of directors of the Brockville YMCA. She lives in Merrickville, Ontario with her partner, Michael.